CHAMPIONS IN THE MAKING

BOOK ONE: Building Positive Self-Concept In Kids

(formerly titled **BREAKFAST FOR CHAMPIONS**)

J. ZINK, Ph.D.

OTHER PUBLICATIONS ON CHILD DEVELOPMENT

BY DR. ZINK:

CHAMPIONS IN THE MAKING
BOOK TWO: Motivating Kids (J. ZINK, INC., 1983)

CHAMPIONS IN THE MAKING
BOOK THREE: Ego States (J. ZINK, INC., 1986)

CHAMPIONS ON THE SCHOOL BUS: A SCHOOL BUS DRIVER'S
GUIDE TO POSITIVE DISCIPLINE ON THE SCHOOL BUS (J. ZINK,
INC., 1982).

CHAMPIONS IN THE LIBRARY: A LIBRARIAN'S GUIDE TO
POSITIVE DISCIPLINE IN THE LIBRARY (J. ZINK, INC., 1982).

CHAMPIONS IN THE MAKING: A POSITIVE APPROACH TO
DISCIPLINE (AUDIO TAPE) J. ZINK, INC., 1982.

A POSITIVE APPROACH TO DISCIPLINE (VIDEO TAPE) J. ZINK,
INC., 1982.

THE COMPLETE CHAMPIONS WORKSHOP (AUDIO TAPES) J.
ZINK, INC., 1986.

CATCH 'EM
DOING SOMETHING
RIGHT!

Dr. J. ZINK

FIRST PRINTING, AUGUST, 1981
SECOND PRINTING, FEBRUARY, 1982
THIRD PRINTING, SEPTEMBER, 1982
FOURTH PRINTING, AUGUST, 1983
FIFTH PRINTING, OCTOBER, 1984
SIXTH PRINTING, APRIL, 1987
SEVENTH PRINTING, MAY, 1988
EIGHTH PRINTING, OCTOBER, 1988

ISBN 0-942490-01-0

Special thanks to Len and Janet Davis for typing and printing this book.

Printed in U.S.A.

This Book is For

JOE ZINK,

And his children
And theirs

PROLOGUE TO THE FIRST EDITION

My father has done an outstanding job in writing a book in a field where no one has taken charge. He writes about raising children better than anyone I know. This book entitled **Breakfast For Champions** is so easy to read I believe a seven-year old child could read it. In fact, if the teachers or parents reading this book have trouble they should give it to their children and have the children teach them. **Breakfast For Champions** is witty and certainly not boring to read. My father included a number of valuable activities to help you better relate to your children.

I can honestly say after thirteen years under my father's plan, I cannot find one fault in it. I can't think of saying thank-you any other way than, "I love you, J."

Please remember to order my father's next book **What To Do When Your Champion Is Out To Lunch**.

Joe Zink
Grade Seven
Center School
Manhattan Beach
California
June, 1981

PROLOGUE TO THE FOURTH EDITION

This book and I have traveled many miles since it was first published two years ago.

Perhaps the greatest joy the work has given me has been meeting parents and teachers all over the world who read this book, freely quote from it, and have underlined or highlighted their favorite passages.

Of course, I love the mail this book generates. Every day someone writes with a tale or two of how they caught a kid doing something right. My favorite story regarding the power of positive messages comes from a woman in Minnesota. She told of her thirty-year marriage to a man who never put his dirty socks in the hamper until the day after she read this book and promised him, in exchange for his socks in the hamper, a KISS.

J. Zink, Ph.D.
Manhattan Beach,
California
June, 1983

TABLE OF CONTENTS

Part One:

THE IDEA

"There is one who gives liberally,
   yet he grows richer, and one
      who withholds what he should give
     and suffers want."

Proverbs 11-24

Chapter One:

THE FORMULA FOR POSITIVE SELF-CONCEPT

This book pretends to be nothing more than a "how-to" manual for building positive self-concept in children and young adults. The language I have chosen to use here is as simple and jargon free as possible. Also, by using the word "formula" in the title of this first chapter, I do not wish to imply that I have a startling new discovery to offer parents and teachers about their kids; however, there is, upon strong examination, an obvious formula for building in kids a positive way of thinking about themselves. Such positive thinking leads to self-confidence, high self-esteem, cheerful "can-do" attitudes, and general success and happiness in life.

I am not a theoretician. I am a successful teacher and parent. If you are looking for some special new theory or revelation about human behavior, look elsewhere. Libraries are filled with treatises on child development. Some are extremely engaging; others are so poorly conceived that they cannot provide answers to simple questions like "why is he so moody?" or "why does she pout when I tell her to do something?" or "why does he insist on teasing his sister?"

Every child comes to know the world through a series of continuous experiences with the people in it. As a child grows, she/he experiences more people. Even minor experiences like buying ice cream from the lady behind the counter or saying hello to a friend, provide the child with important information about him/herself. If we think of this information as continuous and never ending, we begin to understand that this constant diet of messages provides the basic nutrition which feeds a child's self-concept. (Admittedly, by using words like "diet, nutrition, and feeds" I am creating a metaphor. I do so because it is the best way I know to describe the process of self-concept growth.) To continue the metaphor—a child who is given food of little nutritional value will suffer physical (and mental) deterioration; a child who is given nutritious food will grow and develop to his/her potential. (Some say we are what we eat; I say we are, in part, what we are fed.)

For instance, children who are continually praised for their ability to read will soon form a self-concept which clearly **includes** the skill of reading. This happens because a series of messages given by parents and teachers help these children to regard the act of reading as pleasurable, exciting, delightful, and a **good** thing to do. Through this act they experience success. Thus, the skill of reading becomes part of a child's internal picture. When this happens, we can say that the child's own message system has grown to the degree that she/he can deliver his/her own positive messages of engaging in a specific behavior. Most teachers and parents, who have serious trouble with children, forget that with children the messages about pleasure, joy, achievement, excitement, etc., of reading (or any other behavior) **must come from us first**. The formula, then, is simple.

POSITIVE IN/POSITIVE OUT

As a practical example of the formula (Positive In/Positive Out) let us look at a ten-year old boy whose room is constantly a mess. Let us further assume he has the basic abilities to hang clothes in the closet; neatly arrange toys and games; return books to shelves; order rock, bottle cap, baseball card, and stamp collections, make his bed, and, in general, attend to all those specific behaviors necessary to maintain a neat room.* The problem is, as

---

*Of course, some basic inclinations and abilities in a given child must be present for the formula to work. It is highly unlikely that a child who suffers serious and permanent neurological impairment will ever form a self-concept which **includes** strong reading skills. The real danger, however, lies with the parent or teacher who makes a prejudgment about a child's inclination and abilities before sending positive messages regarding certain skills. When we say, "Well, he will never be able to . . ." we err seriously.

most parents of ten-year olds will tell you, he doesn't do any of the above.

What often ensues is a series of messages between parents and son about the room. When analyzed **most** of these messages contain **other** messages about the **person** for whom they are intended.

Father:　　　　　"You call this a room, this is a direct hit!" Message: you are a holocaust.

Mother:　　　　　"Aren't you embarrassed to live like this?" Message: you should feel guilt.

Father:　　　　　"This is a sty! Do you see the rest of us living like this? When I was your age I lived in the same room with two other brothers! You live in your own private palace and you treat it like a garbage dump!" Message: you are garbage.

Mother:　　　　　"I refuse to go in that closet without a tetanus shot. Actually, I am afraid of what I might catch." Message: You scare me.

This reaction from parents, when it produces no permanent results, frequently degenerates into shouts, threats, angry statements, and further strong messages implying that something is wrong with the kid because he chooses to live according to his own needs and not according to his parents.

In order to turn off the heat, this boy might become a "stuffer." All items, including matchbox cars, rubberbands for his braces, geode, one sock, gum eraser, Steve Garvey "doubles," and other treasures get shoved behind drawers, in back of the bed, behind the stereo, and the closet becomes his last stand.

The total breakdown of communication and major dramatic scene comes the day his father is searching for tennis balls and ventures into "the closet" to discover the odor seeping from the piles. Then comes the anger, threats, lectures, tears, emotional statements—the whole closet climax.

Well, it doesn't have to be that way. Again the formula: Positive In/Positive Out. If the goal is for the ten-year old to internalize neatness—that is, to be uncomfortable himself when he walks into a messy room—the place for the parents to begin is with direct communication. They could try: "We want you, Brian, to hang all clothes in the closet, put all books on the shelves, place all underwear in the drawers, or, if dirty, in the dirty clothes hamper. We want no fuzz or bits of paper on the floor."

Now comes the critical step. Remember the formula says "Positive In" first. So keep an "eagle eye" for Brian's first response to your specific message. As soon as he puts books on their shelf say: "Brian, thank you for putting your books on the shelf." Now, look him in the eye and **mean** it. Don't say: "Yeah, you got the books but you forgot your underwear on the floor." (This is very typical of most parents.) Instead say: "Brian, I am delighted that you thought enough of my wishes that you responded so quickly." Don't say: "Nice going champ, but your closet still smells." Say: "Brian, I realize that it takes extra effort to put things away and that you put in the effort for me. Thank you, son. I love it." And put some **passion** into it. If you are not authentic in your praise of kids, they will know it immediately and they will never respect you.

When I say "Positive In," I mean positive in every sense of the word. If what you say is **positive** in your mind, but is interpreted by the child to be **other** than positive, then trouble may be the result. One nice thing about "Positive In" is that it is so pleasant to be with people who are positive.

And, if you are with a positive person, your comfort is assured. Positive people do not threaten nor do they intimidate for the sake of winning at the expense of someone else. Truly positive people do not find joy in winning-at someone else's expense. Remember, if you win at the expense of your child's self-concept, you have lost. Period!

We cannot discount the powerful impact of emotions in the first part of the formula "Positive In." The more positive messages that children receive, the more they will begin to regard themselves in terms of those positive messages. For instance, let us return to Brian. After his parents have taken the time to convey **their specific needs** to Brian and they have taken the pains to carefully send him messages of goodwill and joy regarding his respect of those needs, Brian begins to understand them as people. Brian begins to realize that he can make them happy by simply putting his books away and storing his underwear or toys in their proper places. After a while, (with kids whose negative self-concepts have not been deeply embedded—this time is very short, perhaps three or four days, a week, maybe two) Brian begins to think of himself as a **neat** person.

A word about non-verbal language is also in order (a subject discussed in-depth in later chapters). Parents and teachers often forget that up to 80 % of the messages we send children are non-verbal. The point is that children learn from infancy to communicate non-verbally. It takes them several years to learn what the sounds we make with our mouths mean and several more years to understand what these black marks on a white page mean. But, from birth, children are learning non-verbally.

So remember the formula—Positive In/Positive Out. If your children at home or in your classroom are scowling at you, it may be that you are scowling at them. If, when you draw near them, their eyes narrow, or more significantly, their pupils contract, they have learned these behaviors from **you** and your body language. Change your non-verbal messages from negative to positive and use these to reinforce your positive verbal messages to kids. Smiles in particular are powerful non-verbal positives. And I mean sincere smiles, not "ah-ha, I got you now!" smiles. Try warm and sincere messages which say, **"I care about you."** Winks, laughter, loving pats; handshake between father and teenage son, baseball handslapping of victory, are all expressions of affection and caring. These positive messages will return **from** your kids. When they do—"Positive Out"—it is a sign that the child has not only observed and received your positive messages but that she/he feels sufficiently confident to send them back.

Now, as with all new skills, sending positive messages to kids takes practice. And, when attempting to communicate positively with a child who has a negative self-concept, you cannot charge in glad-handing and backslapping, winking and smiling all the while. It will not work. Worse, it will backfire and serve to alienate further the young person. With some it will serve to reinforce the persistent notion among the young that older people are weird, parents are square, principals are wacko and teachers are manipulators not to be trusted. Go gently at first. Send sincere messages and if you don't mean them, don't send them. Kids read us the way we read books. If your "Positive-In" is not sincere or is overdone, you can forget about "Positive-Out."

Now a final word about the formula. The jaundiced eye might look at this formula and say: "Fine. All you will do is teach kids how to please you and ultimately manipulate you for their own ends."

My response to this worthwhile objection to the formula has two parts. In the first place, positive messages coming back to us from kids are the ultimate tests that the formula is working. If those messages are not authentic, then we can observe a gross discrepancy between what the kids say and what they do. Second, if the kids are so accomplished that they can match their positive words and body messages to us with positive action, then we are seeing either positive self-concept ("I told you I would get an 'A' on my next math test and here it is!") or we are witnessing a young person exercising his/her **new** skills at interacting and communicating. Both of these latter alternatives are exciting for parents and teachers to see.

NOTES

Chapter Two:

THE NEED FOR POSITIVE INFORMATION

Children are born with a non-existent or very, very fragile sense of who or what they are. Infants who are ignored but fed regularly—who are deprived of loving caresses or who are given no stimulation—often die. Older children who suffer repeated rejection may build very strong defenses around themselves for protection against rejection. Some of them commit suicide when their defenses cave in. These, of course, are extreme cases, but they are not rare.

Fortunately, most children receive sufficient attention to keep them alive. If the attention is essentially positive, then they will formulate a generally positive image of themselves and they will begin to feel good about themselves. If the attention is too little and infrequent, then they will experiment to determine what they must do to get attention. Stimulation of any kind is better than none at all and some children learn that disruption and socially maladaptive behavior is extremely adaptive for their main need—attention. These children will not hesitate to cry in church, scream in the airplane, throw mashed potatoes in the restaurant, or stick their finger in their little brother's eye. All these behaviors very quickly achieve their purpose—attention. In the latter case, the eye poking behavior achieves a double purpose because little brother deserves a good poke since he's been the target for all the available attention anyway.

Mother frequently scolds with words like, "You have been nothing but trouble all day!" Unfortunately self-concepts are built on such observations. A child whose need for attention is gratified first by the attention and then by an observation confirming a suspicion that the only way to get anyone to notice is to raise a little hell soon thinks of himself/herself as an effective hell-raiser. In later years, she/he may proudly sport a tatoo that proclaims "born to raise hell."

In very simple terms, self-concept is the mental picture we have of ourselves. It includes things like our names, our backgrounds, our experiences, our sense of right and wrong, our sense of God—(or the ultimate power), our understanding of love and rejection and other powerful emotions, such as what we consider "right" for us in terms of friends, ideas, cars, clothes, music, education and many, many other aspects of our lives that **help us to make decisions**.

The process of self-concept development and the process of how we make decisions about our behavior are very difficult to separate. Although philosophers may well argue distinctions, let us, as parents and teachers, for the sake of understanding our children, presume that a youngster's self-concept and perception of him/herself plays a major part in his/her actions.

I submit that a fifteen-year old boy who thinks of himself as a well-liked and respected student with good interpersonal skills, upon being told to do something "or else," will never, I repeat, never flash his eyes and say, "mess with me and I'll kick your butt."

The boy who says the above to his teacher, especially out loud and in front of his friends, is the product of years and years (fifteen to be exact) of self-concept formation from essentially negative and destructive information. This is a child who has been cuffed and kicked, threatened repeatedly, and often pointlessly punished. This is a child who has been neglected and shunted aside; a child for whom excuses have been made. Clearly in the words of the nursery rhyme, this is "Thursday's child" whose self-concept will allow him to make the decision to be publicly defiant, verbally abusive, and physically threatening. Teacher, mom and dad, **where do you think he learned it?**

With this boy, the formula we discussed in Chapter One, "Positive In/Positive Out," works inside out. "Negative In/Negative Out" very well describes this youngster. Remember, the next time you are faced with unhappy confrontation that the child you are confronting is merely acting out a script which has been handed him/her for years. You **can** change the script. You **do** have the power to change the lines and affect the outcome of the play. You can feed a child junk food and very well expect a sickly child; you can feed a child nutritiously and very well expect a healthy youngster. Give a kid a steady diet of specific positive encouragement and you can very well expect a champion.

Let's discuss how the process of positive self-concept building works.

Children learn our expectations of them chiefly through what it is they do that gets our attention. This is what some educators who advocate reinforcement systems like happy faces, marbles in a jar, and M&M's do not understand about kids. The happy faces, bonus points, marbles, tickets, etc., are a very minor part of the reward/achievement process.

The Congressional Medal of Honor, for example, is only a pretty ribbon and a piece of metal, but it takes on great significance when the President (authority symbol) presents one to you before a joint session of the Congress of the United States. When we (authority symbols) take our own time to stop the normal flow of events to observe that a child has distinguished him/herself by a particular behavior, we have said "I noticed you." We have said, "You are important, special in a certain way." "You mean something special to me." When these messages of sincere emotion are tied plainly and obviously to a specific behavior, then the likelihood of that behavior occuring again, particularly in our presence, is enormous. Kids, like all of us, desire to be recognized, loved, cared for, worried about, squeezed, hugged, helped, praised, admired, respected, and accepted. We all do things which we believe will earn us these things from **ourselves** as well as others. As we learn which **specific** behaviors earn us this respect for ourselves, as well as others, these **specific** behaviors become synonymous with the mental picture we have of who we are. It is how we learn what makes us feel good about ourselves.

Our job, as parents and teachers, is to teach children and young adults how to feel good about themselves for engaging in behavior that will serve them well throughout their lives.

NOTES

Chapter Three:

DEVELOPING A POSITIVE MESSAGE SYSTEM: AN ECOLOGICAL APPROACH

There are three distinct sources of self-concept building messages in the life of a school-age child or young adult. Each of these may be considered a separate ecology. The first of these, from a teacher's standpoint, is the relationship between the teacher and the child. The quality of this relationship is largely determined by the teacher. She/he can watch for appropriate behavior and reward it or she/he can watch for inappropriate behavior and verbally or non-verbally make the child or young adult aware that she/he is acting inappropriately. Whichever the teacher chooses to spot (what is right or what is wrong) has a lot to do with how the child responds to the teacher, and it has a great deal to do with the quality of their relationship.

Adults tend to avoid other adults who offer constant criticism. The same is true of kids. However, in school, kids often have no choice. They are forced to be in a room with a teacher who is constantly critical. Compounding this negative circumstance, their self-concepts are in an extremely formative stage. Thus, a barrage of criticism may force them to retreat within themselves and form a negative picture of themselves complete with a lack of self-confidence, fear of failure, and an overriding sense of their own short-comings. These feelings, naturally, are reflected in their behavior which tends to confirm suspicions that someone else is the star and they are not.

One frequent response to an inunadation of negative messages is defiance. Convinced that his/her role is that of "troublemaker," this powerful youngster will challenge teachers and school administrators. These kids, then, may be convinced they are a "star" of a sort. They think of themselves as skillful disruptors. Unfortunately, it not only enables them to achieve attention from parents and teachers but also earns them the adulation of their friends.

In the extreme, a defiant childs develops a "get-even"

outlook. This revengeful child says, in effect, "Nobody does this to me." Turning this negative self-concept into a positive one takes time, patience, understanding and all those other cliche's that psychologists so often use. It also takes a solid control of all the ecologies (potential source of information) in the kid's life.

Teachers who take the time to look for the strengths of a child and sincerely praise those strengths find their relationship with the student greatly strengthened, the student's performance improved, and the student's self-concept sufficiently strong to occasionally endure failure. Failure is always a learning experience to be sure, but when a student with a strong self-image experiences failure, this student can correct or overcome the problem because this student has learned that failure is not permanent. And failure, under the supervision of a positive teacher and an encouraging parent, is how the maturation process works best. On the other hand, a student with a poor self-concept experiences failure as basically a confirmation of his/her worst suspicions about him/herself.

Within the context of what I am calling the first ecology, teachers, then, must strive to build a positive self-image in their students by consistently rewarding appropriate behavior. When a student feels good about him/herself, then the first source of self-concept building messages has done its job. A major problem here, of course, is that teachers may be aware of this process but they may not have received the specific training they need to send the quality and quantity of messages that children and young adults need to build positive self-images.

The second ecology is the relationship between parents and kids. Here again the quality of this relationship is determined by the authority figure. Parents who take little or no interest in their offspring or who vigilantly point to everthing they do not like are sending messages that cannot possibly contribute to positive self-concepts in their children.

Generally speaking, disinterested parents produce reactionary children. Overly critical parents produce insecure and tremendously unhappy children who frequently spend their lives in search of someone who will validate their self-esteem. As with teachers, parents who produce children with a positive self-concept, with "can-do" and "go get' em" attitudes, do so by consistently praising specific behaviors. As these children experience success and hear how important their achievements are to the most important people in their lives, they form a self-concept which clearly includes all those items for which they have been praised and from which they have experienced the joy of achievement and success.

Of course, the same major problem for teachers exists for parents. They have not been trained to look for what is right in their children, nor have they been trained to respond appropriately when they observe these behaviors. So even though these wonderful behaviors which portend success in life may be present in the child, no one tells the child that what she/he is doing is great. So these behaviors for greatness go away.

The third and final source of self-concept building messages is one which more often than not baffles and mystifies the authority figures in the first two ecologies. For this source, the most powerful of all, is the child's or young adult's peers. Very little of worth has been written about this third ecology. Yet, in many ways, it is the most important. When our children are small, we encourage them to develop friendships and good social skills because as parents and teachers we know the importance of these skills throughout their lives. Yet in many cases when our children pick friends and come under their influence, we are frightened or intimidated because it seems that we have no control over the behavior of our children's friends.

We must recognize that peer pressure, peer approval, and the need for peer acceptance are extraordinary forces in the lives of our kids. Unfortunately, peers often encourage and reward the wrong behaviors in our children.

We also must recognize that the third ecology can be substantially controlled by parents and teachers. Initially, parents must monitor the influences that their children's friends have over them. Certainly this is not a new suggestion. However, **what** to look for is more important than **who** to look for. Parents should realize that their children's friends (like it or not) play a major role in building their children's self-concepts. Parents need to ask themselves two questions. What kind of messages are being sent to my children by their friends? And, what kind of behavior is being rewarded?

In other words, are my children's friends helping to build a positive self-image for my children or are they bossy, critical, overbearing, and negative? (To name just a few cripplers of a positive self-concept.) Or, are they warm, encouraging, and supportive of behavior that you think is **wrong** for your son or daughter? (Behaviors like using illegal drugs, excessive alcohol, and being sexually promiscuous.)

I want to assure you that parents **do** have more control over these positive and negative aspects of the interpersonal environment than they normally acknowledge and there are many things to say, do, and listen for, which will be discussed in later chapters, which can make a difference in the quality of their children's lives and the formation of their children's self-concepts.

The same control is true for teachers. Teachers have more control over peer interaction among their students than they often realize. Teachers who will not tolerate students physically or psychologically abusing each other help to create a positive environment for learning. Gifted teachers, for example, frequently structure classroom activities so that their students are working for a common goal or reward. As the students participate in the achievement of a common reward, they encourage each other to work harder on the team. This kind of positive, work-oriented, creative, achievement-prone environment stimulates positive peer pressure. In a "work for the common good" environment, a student's friends are encouraging him/her to work hard. Rewards such as extra story time, extra games, raffle prizes, etc., (for elementary age children) or reduced homework, no weekend homework, music during art class, etc. (for secondary and middle school youngsters), carry a double reinforcing effect of being a reward by the teacher or school and being greatly desired by the students as a group. Positive group identities form as a direct result of positive interaction between members of the group. This helps to form the positive identities of the individual group members.

Especially skillful teachers, who have mastered the art of engineering peer teaching in their classrooms, are aware that peer teaching is often as much as 30 % more efficient at teaching a lesson than is the teacher alone. There are two reasons for this. Kids speak each other's "language" and few things in life are as important to a child or young adult as properly responding when his/her friend says "do it."

The total ecological approach to positive self-concept

building in kids is best achieved by the close team-work of parents and teachers. At the first sign of trouble (disruption at school, defiance, refusal to do school work, homework, etc.), the parents and teachers involved must sit down and share information and together plan a strategy to help each other stop the inappropriate behavior and begin to focus specifically on the opportunities for sending the child powerful, positive messages about his/her behavior at home and/or at school. In addition, both parents and teachers must discuss, openly and frankly, the specific influences the child's friends have and what steps must be taken to ensure that peer reinforcement is coming for the right reasons.

The specific skill here is the ability of parents and teachers to communicate effectively and not fall prey to blaming postures which bring defenses, guilt, fear of inadequacy, and other items destructive to the specific purpose of the critical parent/teacher meeting.

The general skill is to be **positive**. Realize that each party is experiencing a certain amount of anxiety over the meeting and its cause and quickly get to the business of how you can work together to make sure that Sarah, Deborah, Michael, or Jose' is feeling good about himself/herself for coming to school on time, getting work completed, cooperating with classmates, etc. Furthermore, it is a good idea for each of you to agree on what specific **action** will be taken if the trouble continues and for both of you to clearly communicate this message to the kid. (The need for this type of action, loss of privileges, time-out, detention, suspension, etc., will be reduced in direct proportion to the success of your mutual **positive** plans of action.)

NOTES

Part Two:

THE SKILLS

"He that answereth before he heareth
showeth himself to be a fool and
worthy of confusion."

Proverbs 18, 13

Chapter Four:

POSITIVE LISTENING

Many parents and teachers don't listen! As strange as it may seem, the first important skill to master if you are going to build a positive self-concept in a young person is called positive listening. You ask, "How can something as ostensibly passive as listening help build a positive self-concept in a kid?"

This question can be answered easily when one realize that there is nothing **passive** about positive listening. On the contrary, positive listening is actively observing all the positive aspects of what our kids say and do. By "listenting" I mean using **all** our senses to collect as much information as we can about our children and students. This includes what we hear with our ears, see with our eyes, smell (what is that funny smoke?) with our noses, and intuit with that parent/teacher sixth sense that we all seem to have.

Let's look at an example of a parent who doesn't listen:

Parent: Oh, you are wearing your new tennies. (Van's, Off-The-Wall, special slip-on super grip deck shoes—$23.95 at this writing.)

Son: Aren't they hot? I just love them.

Parent: Do they fit?

Son: These are such a super birthday gift. Thank you very much.

Parent: You're welcome. I'm glad you like them.

Son: These are so hot! (Hint: "hot" means very socially acceptable.) They are the thing to have at school. And, speaking of school, I'm going to be late. Catch you later.

Because the parent in the above dialogue lacked "active listening" skills (the new buzz word in communication training), the parent missed the fact that she/he did not get an answer to a very critical question, "Do they fit?" As all parents of thirteen-year olds will tell you, the fit of the shoe is a critical item because a too-snug fit today means another $23.95 tomorrow.

Advocates of "active listening" skills will say that with practice (and bitter experience!), it is easy and rewarding to **actively** participate in conversations with children—to listen for what they **do not say** or **do not answer** in order to learn to better communicate with them.

So consider the same situation with a parent who is an "active listener"—a real Sherlock Holmes.

Parent: Oh, you are wearing your new tennies!

Son: Aren't they hot? I just love them.

Parent: Do they fit?

Son: These are such a super birthday gift. Thank you very much.

Parent: You're welcome. But do they fit?

Son: These are so hot!

Parent: David, you did not answer my question. Why are you avoiding my question?

Son:　　　　　　(With slight coloration of guilt and
　　　　　　　　protesting.) They fit fine.

Parent:　　　　　Let me feel your toe. (Does so.) Your
　　　　　　　　toe is up to here. These don't fit. They
　　　　　　　　will be too small in a week! And you
　　　　　　　　knew it. You were not going to say a
　　　　　　　　word just so your could wear them to-
　　　　　　　　day, and lie. Sit there and lie through
　　　　　　　　your teeth! (So much for a happy
　　　　　　　　birthday.)

I will spare you the rest of the dialogue since I suspect
you have seen this play before—another time, another
theatre.

My point is simple: active listening is **not**
enough—although it is a step in the right direction. Most
parents and teachers, preoccupied with worries, concerns,
the needs of their own lives and the needs of other kids,
rarely actively listen. When they do, so often the results
are negative, because like some super sleuth, they are constantly in an adversarial role with their kids—alert always
to what they are "up to." As in "what are those little devils
up to now?"

The skill of positive listening is comprised of two parts.
First, active listening and close observation. Second,
rigorously seeking the positive values of any given situation to make that experience a positive learning experience for a kid.

Consider the scene one more time.

Parent:　　　　　Oh, you are wearing your new ten-
　　　　　　　　nies!

Son: Aren't they hot? I just love them.

Parent: Do they fit?

Son: These are such a super birthday gift. Thank you very much.

Parent: You're welcome. But do they fit?

Son: These are so hot!

Parent: (Skill one; part one.) David do your tennis shoes fit?

Son: (With slight coloration of guilt and protesting.) They fit fine.

Parent: Let me feel your toe. (Does so.) These don't fit. They will be too small in a week. I understand the situation. You wanted the wear your new tennis shoes to school on your birthday. The thought of wearing your old ones was unattractive. If you wear them today and they get dirty—which they will—we cannot return and exchange them. In a few weeks, they will cramp and hurt your feet. You will not want to wear them. We will all be very upset. (Spells out natural consequences.) What do you think we should do?

Son: (Disappointed and facing reality.) We'll take them back and get a half-size larger. I will wear my old ones today. (Kids can handle disappointment—they can!)

If at this point the parent has been looking for the positive potentials for learning in this situation, she/he should have determined that there is substantial opportunity to teach his/her son the value of family cooperation, that he can survive disappointment, and that he is a responsible member of the family. When a parent detects these kinds of opportunities, she/he is a positive listener.

When these opportunities are realized through "positive talking" (discussed in the next chapter), then parents are on their way to building positive self-concepts in their kids. Stop looking for ways to make them feel bad and start looking for ways to make them feel good.

Consider what happens to David: instead of looking down at new shoes all day and feeling the pain of guilt, knowing that the day of reckoning is not far away, David looks down at his disgraceful, old shoes all day and feels good about himself. He **is** a good person, he thinks as he looks down—"I can handle these shoes one more day." In fact, he's proud of these shoes, for now they carry a special meaning. They are a visable reminder of his sense of responsibility, and that he is a good family member.

Now, the "jaundiced eye" is blinking once again: But the kid lied! He lied! What are you going to do about that? Well, the truth is, he didn't lie, actually. David said, "They fit fine." And they did. But not the right "fine."

But, if this kind of "truth coloration" or bending or shaping of the facts is leading to a serious problem—that

is, overt and frequent lying, then you can (and should) do
something about it. You could tell him, **calmly**, that his lying cost him the use of his bicycle for a week, or some
other appropriate deprivation. But you don't yell, scream,
shout, threaten or otherwise remonstrate unless you wish
to send many negative messages, which I promise, will
soon come back to you.

The point is that a kid who learns to accept disappointment and accept responsibility will not only feel good
about him/herself, but this kid will have no need to lie the
next time a similar situation arises. She/he will learn to feel
good for telling the truth.

Just think of the few extra minutes it takes to **look for**
positive values in our children. Compare this to a lifetime
of misery, worry, and unhappiness caused by a kid with
low self-esteem and a negative self-concept. As a teacher
and counselor, I have said to so many parents who cannot
take the time to be positive, "Mr. and Mrs. Borman, we
have Kristen this year and next; you have her forever!"

Now, let's look at a typical school situation for another
example of positive listening in action. (A private conver-
sation.)

Student: Mrs. Jenkins?

Teacher: Yes, what is it, Stuart?

Student: I can't do this stuff, today.

Teacher: Why?

Student: I'm very upset, today. My parents had
                a big fight last night and I couldn't
                sleep. My dad, he left last night, slam-

med the door. I'm really upset bad.

Teacher: Well, it will blow over. It always does.
                  If you don't feel well today, just sit
                  quietly and don't bother anyone else.

This is a classic case of not listening to the message. A
close look at Stuart's eyes would confirm his lack of sleep.
A close look at his pupils might disclose something about
drug involvement—a sniff of his breath may disclose
something about his involvement with alcohol. But these
things, along with the painful story, are unpleasant and
the easiest thing for the teacher to do is say "just don't
bother anyone else today."

The same situation with a teacher who is an "active
listener" might indeed disclose something of the truth, of
drugs or booze, or a simpler truth: his parents did collide
last night. The active listener without the positive skills
might say, "Parents had a fight, right—about you on
drugs. I'm a teacher with a room full of dilated pupils, and
you have two of them!"

The positive listener, however, would detect the most
significant message. She/he would read Stuart's verbal and
non-verbal behavior as a plea for help—especially at a
time when his security at home has been shaken. The last
response a kid needs whose family life has been disrupted
is a weak and non-supportive "do what you want" from
his teacher.

There are (of course) many avenues for teachers to take
with students like Stuart. Parent involvement, support
from the administration, help from a social worker, training about drug abuse from local law enforcement person-
nel, etc., are all appropriate. But true success of those in-
terventions **all** depend on Stuart recognizing that his

teacher is not **the enemy**. Fortunately, the various subskills of positive listening are easy to learn and yield wonderful results.

ONE

Give the kid your complete attention. Sometimes your complete attention alone is all that the situation requires.

Note of warning: If your complete attention is impossible at the time, i.e., you are busy with another youngster or you are in the middle of a lesson, make a specific time available when you can give your complete attention and **don't break the date**.

TWO

Analyze the kid's non-verbal language. While it is very important to listen to his/her words, remember up to 80% of what she/he is saying is being non-verbally communicated. Look for signs that conflict: often kids will say one thing with their mouths and say the opposite with their bodies. Example: to a direct question while saying "Yes" she/he will shake his/her head "No." If you are worried about the truth, look into his/her eyes. Remember, anyone can lie, but it takes a master—bordering on the pathological—to lie with his/her eyes. And, look for eye contact.* A lack of

*There are cultural variations in eye contact behavior that may need to be considered with ethnic minority children.

eye contact, especially during normal, non-threatening conversations, may be one significant sign of a reduced self-concept.

THREE **Don't make snap judgments.** Listen, observe, and, above all else, stay calm. Hysteria only complicates the healing process and, worse, stupid and sometimes vicious things are said in anger and they can **never** be retracted. Stay cool, mom and dad; stay relaxed, teacher. Children and young adults do not respect people who are always coming unhinged.

FOUR **Listen for what is avoided.** Children and young adults with negative self-concepts will invariably diminish their positive contributions to a particular situation. By recognizing and observing their particular worth and by pointing out to them what they did that was useful, intelligent, caring, etc., you do two wonderful things: 1) you show them their worth in your eyes, and 2) you teach them to look for the positive aspects of problem situations.

FIVE **Overcome your impulse to talk.** This may be the toughest subskill to master in positive listening. As parents and teachers we are programmed to spew information as soon as a kid moves into range. You cannot be a positive listener and talk at the same time.

SIX   **Be vigilant for the positive aspects of
the situation**. Virtually all situations
have their positive aspects. Of course,
this excludes the heinous: ("Didn't that
gun make a surprisingly loud noise
when you pulled the trigger!")

By looking for what is **right** about a kid, we have the
raw material to begin the self-concept building process.
Positive self-concepts take time, energy, patience, and
love to build. They can be damaged in a split second.
When our positive listening yields **good** things about a
kid, we can use those good things to begin a series of
positive messages which will aid the healing process and
start the kid on the road to thinking of him/herself as a
champion. And teacher, mom and dad, like the cereal ad
told us so many times when we were kids ourselves,
"champions are made, not born."

NOTES

NOTES

Chapter Five:

POSITIVE TALKING

Once positive listening has yielded a place to start, then it is time to make a positive response. Unfortunately and for a lot of reasons, many parents and teachers are seriously deficient at this critical skill. Certainly few parents and, surprisingly, few teachers have been trained in the use of effective positive reinforcement. Those who have received some kind of "behavior modification" training often fail to realize (maybe because of a self-concept problems themselves), how supremely important their emotional responses are to kids. Kids want to know we feel good about them. They constantly study us watching for signs of approval. Winks, smiles, warm hellos, pats, hugs, playful teasing, joking, and sharing "secrets" are all part of the interpersonal intimacies of acceptance and love that kids crave. They want to share their lives and their feelings with us. They want so much to be accepted and not condoned, proud and not embarrassed, victorious and not defeated.

Talking positive is the way to begin to reach out and connect with kids whose self-concepts need help. But first, for the purposes of contrast, let's consider the following negative situations:

Student: Does this mean I scored the highest grade in the clsss?

Teacher: Don't let it go to your head.

                    *   *   *   *

Son: Hey, sports fans, look at this report card. Four "A's" and a "B."

Dad: "B"? What did you get a "B" in?

                    *   *   *   *

Daughter: My face is looking so much better
                 since I changed medication.

Mother: Just don't forget to use it or you'll look
                 like a pizza again.

Many times kids hide their need for approval and support behind a mask of bravado. Parents and teachers, who
are not positive listeners, may feel a need to "take them
down a notch or two" out of some unfounded and foolish
fear that they will "get too big for their britches." Parents
and teachers frequently respond to those plain messages
for approval with disapproval—at times laced with sarcasm or even bitter rancor.

What does the father who responds to his son's nearly
perfect report card hope to accomplish by commenting on
its sole imperfection? If he thinks his reaction will
motivate his son to greater achievement, he is unwise.
Achievement is born of self-worth. When it is accompanied by a desire to sting, put down, or "show somebody
a thing or two," it has very nasty side-effects. Champions
who use their power for revenge can be very unpleasant
to live with.

When rancor motivates a parental response, nothing
but trouble results. A mother who responds to her
daughter's thinly-disguised request for encouragement
about her improved acne condition with a scornful
reminder and an insensitive simile hardly can expect her
daughter to seek her counsel and support when she is in
serious trouble.

Most unforgivable is a teacher, whose primary mission
it is to build confidence in kids, verbally slapping down a
child who is really asking "Didn't I do well? Aren't you
pleased with me?" Many teachers say such things as

"Don't let it go to your head" because such one liners entertain the class. This entertainment is costly, indeed. For a student who is derided by peers because of a witty Groucho Marx or Don Rickles line by the teacher has learned a terrible thing—that for the sake of a laugh, or the sense of the power of control, the teacher would hurt him/her. Such teachers may have the air let out of their tires or "super glue" squirted into their car door locks. And it isn't because they are loved and respected.

Contrast this to the teacher who has positive listening and responding skills. Let's consider the first situation again.

Student: Does this mean I scored the highest grade in the class?

Teacher: Yes it does. Your hard work has paid off handsomely. It is an impressive achievement.

Because this teacher positively listened and heard the "notice me" in the student's question, and because this teacher realized that a positive response—sincerely delivered—was a golden opportunity (an "I like what you did"), we can all safely bet that we will see hard work from this student in the future. If a sufficient amount (and this amount varies from kid to kid) of positive response about hard work and academic achievement comes from all the significant others in this kid's life, she/he will form a positive self-concept which **includes** hard work and academic achievement. Once this concept is formed, then the true reward for hard work and academic achievement comes from within.

Consider the second situation.

Son: Hey sports fans, look at this report
                    card. Four "A's" and a "B."

Father: Hey! Fabulous. That's Honor Roll.
                    Paul, this means the Honor Roll! You
                    are looking at one proud father! Wait
                    'til your mother sees this!

Here the father expends no more energy than in our
first example. Yet, because of his words, and because of
his body language which is beaming with pride, his son
has **felt** a totally different response. His son **feels** that jolt
of kinesthetic energy he would feel if he hit the ball out of
the park to win the game and, as he rounded third base,
saw his father jumping up and down in the stands hugging
his mother.

Well, dad, four "A's" and a "B" means that kid has just
cleared the bases in the game of life, and if you miss the
fact that your son has just won the game, and worse, you
say "You call that a home run? It barely squeeked over the
fence," you are well on your way to striking out in your
own game of life. Remember when its late in your own
game and you are many runs behind—he lives in another
city, hasn't called for months, has been in and out of trouble with the law, can't seem to keep a steady
job—remember how you left so many runners stranded
on base in the early innings of the game—remember how
your runner got thrown out because you sent him the
wrong signal.

Now, let's examine the third situation.

Daughter: My face is looking so much better
                    since I changed the medication.

Mother: You deserve the credit for that. You

haven't missed a day of medication. That kind of dedication pays off. I am **thrilled** for you!

Here again is a mother who has detected that her teenage daughter is saying "I'm here, too. I'm doing my best. Right? Isn't that right?" Mother catches an opportunity to **reinforce** the kind of dedication she has observed in her daughter. Her response is a simple, but **very powerful**, "I like you." It has greater value than a new dress (as a reward) for the prom, or a new car, a blank check, or a "shared" master charge (she gets the card/you get the bill).

The feeling of happiness (felt in a sincere response), with no reservations, strings, conditions or other items to diminish the excitement of the moment has a power to do what **material** items can only **symbolize**. Material items can never subsititute for you.

A parent or teacher who is a positive talker seeks always to make a positive, self-concept building response to kids. Of course, this is easy to say and, at times, extremely difficult to do. You will master the art of positive talking if you practice the following subskills of the positive response.

ONE   **Make your body send the same message your mouth is sending.** A kid who is looking into armor-piercing eyes and hearing words chattering like a machine gun through clenched teeth may miss the meaning of "You are doing good work today."

TWO   **Avoid using sarcasm.** Parents and teachers whose habit it is to deliver a message with two meanings often

draw "Do you really mean it?" looks
when they sincerely praise kids. If you
must be sarcastic, confine your
remarks to the subject matter. Never
be sarcastic about kids—never. Parents
who use sarcasm to control children
should be advised that they will be
controlled by the same weapon when
they are the kids and their kids are
their parents. Nursing home conversations are incredibly revealing about
the past.

THREE

**Put some emotion in your positive
response**. Let them know you mean it.
Remember champions thrive on the
applause and adulation of the crowd.
Even if you know in your heart you
are the best and have the most solid
positive self-concept in the world,
there is nothing like being called from
the dugout by a standing ovation.
Nothing like the roses hitting the stage
to cries of "encore!" Nothing like being carried from the field on the
shoulders of your teammates to the
deafening roar of the crowd. Nothing
like reading the telegrams con-
gratulating you on the Pulitzer Prize.
These are the magic moments of life.
How is a kid going to develop a taste
of victory, unless we, who are the first
audience, give him/her a sample of the
sweetness of victory? The more you
yell and scream about something good
the less you will have cause to yell and
scream about something bad. *Note of*

warning: Don't be phony. If yelling and screaming about something good isn't your style, don't do it. But **do something** to let that kid know you think she/he is a star, or she/he may never be one. And if you ever think that not all of us can be stars, spend a few days in a rehabilitation ward for disabled children. Watch a child with no arms feed herself with her feet and then tell me some of us cannot be stars!

FOUR **Single out specific behaviors for praise**. Tie your positive responses to specific behaviors which you want to see in the future. Kids love to find out what it is we expect of them. This gives them a way to get our attention for beneficial rather than destructive activities. The general praise ("I like you") is worthwhile, but it can lose impact quickly. ("I know. I know. You like me already.") Specific praise such as "Jan, when I pass your room and it looks as neat as the Hilton, I feel like I'm doing a good job at being a parent. Thank you" is much more effective because the next time Jan feels a need for a positive response from you she will clean and straighten her room. *Note of warning*: Do not fall into the trap of "please, please me or else." Parents who make their affection and positive responses *conditional* ("If you are home on time, I will love you; if you are not, I will not speak to you for a week") are playing a dangerous game called "power struggle." In this game someone always loses and in parent-child and teacher-student relationships, when one party wins at the other party's expense, **both** parties lose. The "please, please me or else" trap is easily avoided. Sample: "Maria you look stunning. You should have a smashing time tonight! By the way, I expect you home no later than 12:30. If you are going to be a little late, don't have Dennis drive wrecklessly, call and explain. If you do not call and you are not home by 12:30, you're grounded for two weeks **by your own choice**. Now, have a great time. I love you."

FIVE

Once is never enough. Just because you made a big fuss over the fact that he went potty all by himself yesterday is no reason no to make a big fuss today. It will only lose its **meaning** if you don't **mean** it. One father I know has a wonderful solution to the problem of sending repeated positive messages. He would say, after his oldest son had done something particularly unselfish, "Your making points, Mark, you're making points." His son told me it wasn't long before he realized that the points were not being tallied and there was no prize waiting at the end. What he discovered was that "you're making points" was his father's sincere way of telling him, an athlete, that he was winning the game. Futhermore, the son knew that by being unselfish or by giving freely of his time and effort for the betterment of others, he would undoubtedly **attract his father's attention**. When you are the oldest of five children, positive parental attention can be a rare item, and from his father's point of view, having five children is a lot easier when the eldest is "unselfish" and helpful.

SIX

Never give up. The positive effects of your effort to build a positive self-concept in a kid may not be immediately apparent. (Here's a scary thought: the negative effects of your negative and punishing responses are not always immediately apparent, either! Parents and teachers who insist on using corporal punishment, and who defensively point to its effectiveness, are short-sighted. While "paddling" a youngster may very well get him to behave, it also teaches that physical violence is an appropriate response when someone does not do what you tell him/her to do. Makes you wonder why we live in such a violent country, doesn't it?)

Keep at it. There is a positive value and something to be learned by every situation. Oddly enough, this skill of positive persistence is one that many teachers lack. We tend to try something once or twice and then dismiss it if we see no immediate reaction. Remember the sage advice of the English poet, Geoffrey Chaucer: "Life is so short and the craft is so long to learn."

To some up, the skill of positive talking accomplishes a number of important tasks in the process of building a positive self-concept in kids. In the first place, it lets the kids know you like them. Secondly, it helps to communicate your high expectations for them. Third, it teaches kids to be positive in their approach to their own problems. Fourth, it sets a positive tone to your relationships and keeps those lines of communication open. Finally, a positive response is the best defense against the biggest psychological crippler of all kids—"I can't." Motivation is born of a will to do and do well. Champions always say, "Put me in, coach. Just get me on that field. Oh, come on coach, let me at 'em."

If you have done your job well, mom and dad, and if you have consistently responded in a positive and reinforcing way, teacher, there is no feeling which can match the one you get when they ask for the chance to try something new and you say, "GO GET 'EM!"

NOTES

Part Three:

PRACTICE

"It is better to be invited to herbs with
love than to a fatted calf with hatred."

Proverbs 15, 17

Chapter Six:

TIPS FOR PARENTS IN TROUBLE

Practicing the skills of positive listening and positive talking will yield good results for parents who previously established positive communication patterns with their children. But what about these skills and their effectiveness when the parent-child relationship is rocky or has gone sour? How can a parent in trouble build a positive self-concept in a kid when their history has been solid stream of negative information about each other?

Here are four tips for parents in trouble. By following the suggestions in the tips, studying the illustrations, and completing the exercises, you will begin to practice the principles on which this book is based. *Note of warning*: You must believe in yourself and believe you have the power to change the kind and quality of messages you are sending your youngster. If you do not believe you can change, you are wasting your time reading this book. If you believe you cannot change yourself, how can you possibly change a kid? It is so much easier to raise winners when you act like a winner yourself.

TIP ONE   Take Honest Stock of Yourself.

Sit down in a quiet, reflective moment and take a brutally honest look at who you are, what you believe in, and what you do to support or supplant those beliefs. Are you a "do as I say, not as I do" parent? Do you rant on a soapbox about drugs to your kids and then down three martinis at the end of the day? Do you get upset when your kids are suspended from school for smoking when you are still on two packs a day? Do you worry about what foods your children are eating when you are carrying thirty pounds more than you should and never watch TV without "munchies"? Do you want loving, long-lasting, and wonderfully reinforcing relationships for your children someday, when you are "in the process" of divorce number four?

These are tough questions, mom and dad, but they must be asked not by me, but by you of yourself. Because it is very hard to help your children decide what is "right" for them, if it is obvious to them that you do not know what is "right" for you. If you are like the rest of us, your self-assessment will turn up a number of areas in your personal life which need attention. And, you cannot fix them all overnight. So, pick out one, one that **is** fixable, and work on it. Furthermore, let everybody in the family **know** you are working on it. They will help support you as you change. Now, instead of telling your kids how to live their lives, you are **showing** them—modeling for them—how an adult tackles a tough problem and **wins**.

Illustration For Tip One

Steven, a seventeen-year old high school drop-out and his father, Peter Smith, an insurance executive, had a terrible and hateful relationship. Peter on Steven: "Kid is into drugs. Nothing heavy, mostly marijuana, has a girl and he spends all his time at her place. Dropped out of high school—even though he had good grades. When he smart-mouthed me, I used to work him over good, but now he's bigger than I am and about a year ago he really cleaned my clock. Can't wait until he's eighteen and I can throw him out. A damn shame you know, kid is awfully bright." Steven on Peter: "He comes home, has a few drinks, and first thing you know he's on my case. Usually it's well, if you're not in school, then get a job. You think I want to end up like him? Fat, over forty, and stuck on a treadmill kissing up to somebody all day? Don't get me wrong, my dad's not a bad guy, he's just a jerk sometimes."

It was clear that both father and son wanted their relationship to be different but neither knew where to begin. When Peter took a good look at himself, he realized that he hadn't set a very good example for Steven to follow. So the first thing he did was cut out hard alcohol. The second thing he did, at my suggestion, was to start a light jogging and exercise program before work everyday. After nearly a month, he had lost nine pounds and told me he never felt better in his life. I suggested he invite Steven to run with him in the mornings after making a pact with Steven that during workouts they would send **no** negative messages to each other. Steven told me later that those first couple of days were awfully quiet mornings, but later they talked about "safe" subjects like the weather and the morning air. Peter told me privately that he almost fell over the day Steven told him, "You run pretty well for an old guy." Ultimately Steven finished a GED (high school equivalency diploma) and went to college.

Exercise For Tip One

Complete the following self-assessment. It will give you insight into your own self-concept. Score 10 points for a "yes" answer, 5 points for a "sometimes" answer, and 0 for a "no."

Score 100	you're lying
75-95	you're okay
50-70	shakey
below 50	get your act together

1.   Do I live by an established and consistant set of rules?

2.   Do I periodically revise my set of rules when it is prudent and appropriate to do so?

3. Do I refuse to **force** my values and standards for my own life on other members of my family?

_____

4. Do I look at both sides of an issue, and do I look at **positive** outcomes for each course of action?

_____

5. Can I control my anger and do I have the strength to restrain rage?

_____

6. Do I respond positively to genuine and well-intended criticism?

_____

7. Can I accept lifestyles which are different from my own?

_____

8. Do I look for positive value in other people's solutions to problems we have in common?

_____

9. Do I ask the same behavior of my children that I expect from myself?

_____

10.   Do I stay cool under fire when I am
             challenged by my children?

             _____

A final comment about Tip One: Taking Honest Stock of Yourself. If your current score shows need for improvement, pick an area and go to work. Then re-do the above exercise in three months. If by that time your score has improved, and you have been honest, then I guarantee your relationship with your kids has improved. For those of you who have trouble with self-deception, ask another member of your family to "check" your answers. You may be astonished at the results.

TIP TWO   **Learn to Accept What You Cannot
                   Change and Look for Positive Value
                   in it.**

If you have made a decision to raise children as a divorced single parent, then live with that decision and do not be racked with guilt every time the kids do something you don't like. That guilt and the compensations you make because of it will begin to show in your relationships with your kids. Learning to accept what you can't change is an important step toward feeling good about yourself as a person. It is difficult to act like a champion when you feel guilty about something you have done. When you are crippled with self-doubt about a course of action, you will send conflicting and inconsistent messages to your kids. It is very hard to look for positive values in your youngsters when you are unhappy yourself.

Illustration For Tip Two

Tanya, age fifteen, finally told her parents that she was pregnant. She refused to disclose the father, partly because of a fear of what her father might do to the boy and partly because she wasn't sure which one of three possible boys was the father. Her mother was very helpful. All she did was cry.

When Tanya would come into the room, her mother would start to cry. When she did say anything, she said through tears, "How could you do this to us?" and "What did we do to deserve this?" Tanya's father was even more helpful. He referred to Tanya's unborn baby as "the little bastard" and to Tanya as a "slut." It isn't a wonder why Tanya got herself in this mess in the first place. Clearly, her self-concept was in such bad shape from the negative messages her parents had been sending her over the years that she found herself in the comforting arms of the first three boys who paid her any positive attention. Sexual promiscuity and a diminished self-concept are old friends.

The thing to be learned here is what's done is done, and Tanya's parents must accept it. To further send negative messages will not solve this problem or make the baby go away. The healing and building process must begin, and there is much work to be done. The sad aspect of this case it that since Tanya's parents focused on everything she did that was wrong and failed to build her self-concept, Tanya who is working from her parents as a model, will begin to send the same kind of self-concept destroying messages to her child. Can't you imagine the love and attention "the little bastard" will get at home? It will not be many years before he lives up to his name.

Exercise For Tip Two

I.   Down the left-hand side of a sheet of paper, make a list of all the things your children do that you do **not** like. Down the right-hand side, make a list of all the things they do that you like.

Example

Marla: Age 9

DISLIKE	LIKE
1 Watches TV too much.	1 Goes to bed on time.
2 Waits to the last minute to do her homework.	2 Is courteous; says please and thank you.
3 Does not hang her clothes in the closet.	3 Has good telephone manners.
4 Hates to visit with her father—fights with her stepbrother. Gets scolded by her stepmother.	4 Has good eye-contact when meeting new people.
5 Hates to wear her orthodonture retainer.	

II.   Now think back to how long it took you to write each side of the list. If you are like most parents, you did the left side in seconds; the right side took longer, and you had to think about it. Tells you something, doesn't it?

III.   Look down the right-hand column (things you like) and ask yourself this tough question: How many times, **last**

week, did I praise him/her for one or more of the above? If your answer is **at least once** per item, congratulate yourself on doing a good job building a positive self-concept in your kid. If it isn't **at least once**, then get to work.

IV. Look down the left-hand column (things you don't like) and ask yourself this tough question: How many times last week did we discuss; I yell and scream about; I lose my temper about; I spend hours on the phone talking to my analyst about? Very revealing, isn't it? Do you see how Marla has learned to get your attention?

V. Once more look down the left-hand column (dislike). Which of the five behaviors are you **least** likely to change and have little or (in some cases) **no** control over? I hope you said, "Number four, hates to visit her father, etc." If you did, you are mastering the point of Tip Two: Learn to Accept What You Can't Change. So, look for the positive (skill one) and respond positively (skill two): "Marla, your father has a right, by nature and by civil law, to see you and spend time with you. And he loves you! Life will confront you with difficult people, and you must develop skills to cope with them. So learning to cope with your brother, Marvin, and your father's wife, whom your father loves very much, is great practice for you in the future. I know you are strong and can handle this situation well. I love you, too!"

TIP THREE   **Establish Reasonable and Serious Rules For Your Household and Catch the Kids Following the Rules.**

All effective management systems begin with the rules. The rules for the household are the official by-laws by which **all** members of the household live. Rules of the house are clearly communicated expectations of behavior for all. These rules must be worded very clearly, or the power children in your family will play "lawyer" with you. Example: instead of "no rough-housing" or "no horseplay"—both of which are metaphorical in nature—**get specific**. Example: "no pushing, shoving, kicking, hitting, spitting, or biting, ever." Here are some more examples for specific household rules which families have found useful:

1.   All beds will be made in the morning by the persons who slept in them.

2.   All dirty laundry will be deposited in the dirty clothes hamper by the person who wore it last.

3.   All lights will be turned off by the person who leaves the room last.

4.   The garage door stays closed at **all** times except when in use.

5.   **First** task of the morning. Brush your teeth.

6.   Rubber band retainers for orthodonture appliances found on the floor, floating in the soup, stuck against the ceiling, etc., will cost you $1.00 apiece. Money will be deducted automatically from your savings account, including birthday money.

7.   No one leaves this house without letting someone know, in person, by phone, or by note, 1) where she/he is going to be and, 2) when she/he will return, and if possible, a phone number where we can reach you.

8.   Bedrooms will be dusted, straightened, and swept at least once per week by the person(s) who sleep(s) in them.

9.   All homework will be completed by **no later than** the night before it is turned in.

10.   All homework will be checked and *signed* by a parent before it is turned in.

11.   All arguments will be settled by the persons involved, **peaceably**, unless a house rule has been broken. Then we want to know about it.

12.   All prescriptions and other internal medication is in one place, (medicine cabinet) which is always locked, and mother has the only key.

13.   Kids can consume alcoholic beverages

only in the presence, and with the permission of a parent.

14. Any trouble at school—including being warned or disciplined by a teacher or adminstrator—will be reported to mom or dad the **night** of the day it happened. No exceptions.

15. No one is to take illicit drugs, smoke or eat marijuana, sniff, snort, or inject mind-altering substances; or engage in any activity they would not do in front of mom and dad.

16. **Fire:**   **Get everybody out— take no** personal property. Call the fire department.

Tornado: Go to the basement.

Earthquake: Climb under a table or stand in a doorway; **after** the shaking, go the the middle of the baseball field across the street. Wait until we get there.

17. No one says or does anything to anyone which could possibly hurt his/her feelings.

18. No derogatory nicknames such as: "metal mouth," "elephant breath," "bird brain," "Dolly Parton," etc.

19.   If you can't say something nice or constructive about or to someone, **don't say it**.

20.   Telephones will be answered "**(family name)**" residence. This is "**your name**." To take a message, make a note of the call, including the time, and leave it by the phone in the kitchen.

21.   The person eating or drinking the last of an item will automatically record that item on the kitchen shopping list.

22.   No offensive language in this house.

23.   No teasing which results in hurt feelings or tears.

24.   All pets will be cared for—cages cleaned, fed, watered, bathed, deflead, etc., by their owners and **no one else**.

25.   No loud music after 9:30 PM.

26.   All new friends will spend **at least** one evening at the house getting to know us. **We want to know your friends**.

27.   Be polite. No vulgar animal noises in this house.

28.   Do not wash your hair in the sink. Wash the sink after you use it.

29.   No running or ball playing in the house.

30.   Do not drink soda pop with sugar in it or eat "junk food" with additives, preservatives, or food dyes in them.

Exercise For Tip Three

I.   By yourself or with your spouse, and using the above list as inspiration only, construct **your own list** of house rules using this guideline: keep the list to the absolute **minimum** number needed to run your household. Too many rules are as bad as too few.

II.   Sit down, at a quiet and appropriate time, communicate and discuss the rules with your kids. Answer all questions and clarify all rules which are unclear or fail to communicate your intentions.

III.   Explain what will happen when house rules are broken. (Hint: you'd better do something **every** time the rules are broken, or they will think you don't care about the rules you made.)

IV.   Tell them what will result if they follow the rules. This is the **most important aspect** of your communication. All must understand that very positive and good things will happen as a result of all kids following the rules. Coaches, who are **all** firm believers in training rules (ask one, if you don't believe me), point out frequently to their teams that by following training rules the team will develop team spirit, cohesiveness, a sense of unity and purpose, a winning attitude, and a strong sense of identity—in short, mom and dad, everything you want for your family.

V.   In the first few weeks after you have instituted your rules, **vigilantly** exercise the skills of positive listening and positive talking. By stating the rules, you have set up the perfect opportunity to practice your new skills of watching for opportunities to build the self-concepts of your children. Positive self-concepts are built because kids feel good about themselves for accepting the responsibility for their own behavior. You can start this process of accepting responsibility by 1) giving them rules to live by and 2) pointing out how **well** they are doing. If that sounds like an oversimplification, **it isn't**. You don't have to be a genius or a behavioral scientist to raise champions. You must, however, follow learning theorist Wesley Becker's most famous directive on kids:

"Catch them being good."

By setting rules, you are creating natural opportunities to follow this man's excellent advice.

VI.   Periodically, revise your rules and let everyone know you have done so. As your kids grow, your household will automatically change. If you have done a good job at self-concept building in their early years, their later years will be a pleasure. But never believe that any of us are so mature and responsible that we can live without rules. (Maturity means living by a set of rules.) Rules, particularly ones made by an individual for him/herself, are the quintessential bench-marks of self-discipline. One other point: never forget that kids crave discipline. This is why they will always make tougher rules for their own behavior than we would for them. What better way to say, "I love you," than to say, "I noticed you made your bed. Nice job, Roger. Good going."

TIP FOUR   Whatever Happens, Keep Talking and Don't Give Up.

Ridiculous postures like "Go and never darken our door again" or turning the kid's picture to the wall only serve to hurt and continue to send the negative messages that ruined your relationship in the first place. Thunderous pronouncements of doom and having the lawyers revise the will are always regretted later. Keep those lines of communication open because when kids can't turn to their parents, they turn to someone else. This certainly should explain the astounding number of teenage runaways and the phenomenon of the quasi-religious cults overflowing with young people prepared to adorn themselves in unfamiliar garb and engage in strange and nonsensical behaviors. Everyone needs someone to talk to, mom and dad; if things are very, very bad, do something intelligent and seek professional help. You wouldn't think of treating an infected appendix by yourself; a serious rupture in the family lines of communication can be as deadly as peritonitis. It is a very hard thing to say to you, but parents who bury their overdosed children always say, "If only he had come to me. I didn't realize. My God, I didn't realize."

Ask friends whose judgments you trust for a recommendation; you will be surprised how many of them have sought professional help and received excellent care and valuable, practical advice. If you do not want to ask friends, pick up the yellow pages and look under "marriage and family counselors." Pick out a name, make an appointment, and go. If you don't like that person, pick out another name until you find someone you like, trust, and who can help you re-establish basic communication with your kid. You cannot build a positive self-concept if you are not talking.

Illustration For Tip Four

Delia Paterson was told by the teachers and the school psychologist that her twelve-year old, Delvin, was exhibiting symptoms of "the hyperkinetic syndrome." She had to admit it: Delvin couldn't sit still for ten seconds. She had tried beating him; threatening him; depriving him of television, his bicycle, and his skateboard. He would not sit down and do his homework. Then he started running away from home. Once, he covered twenty miles before a squad car picked him up because they didn't recognize him from their neighborhood. The school psychologist recommended that Delia have Delvin "looked at" by the local pediatrician, who promptly prescribed Ritalin. That certainly stopped the running away. Delvin didn't have the energy to push a pencil. This solution sure made his teacher happy. When Delvin arrived at school, the first thing they asked him was "Did you take your medication today?"

The only person who wasn't happy was Delia Paterson. She noticed Delvin's appetite was poor, and he wasn't growing as fast as he should for his age. So she changed doctors. The new one changed one drug (Ritalin) for another (Cylert). She changed doctors, again. This time she found an education psychologist with a keen interest in nutrition. He recommended discontinuation of the medication, hair analysis, and the basic diet recommended for children by Lendon Smith, M.D., in his exceptional book, *Feed Your Kids Right* (McGraw Hill, 1979). The hair analysis revealed that Delvin was suffering from iron and zink [sic] deficiencies. In addition, his body needed far larger quantities of vitamins C and D than he was getting. The new diet (no sugars, no additives, no preservatives, no food dyes, whole grains, white cheeses, peanuts, fish, chicken, fresh vegetables, and very low sodium) effected a major change in Delvin's behavior. Now, with encouragement and a lot of positive information about his achievements, Delvin was able to sit down and do his homework at one sitting for **the first time in his life**. All this because a mother persisted. Now she was in a position to keep talking because Delvin was in a position to listen and respond. It is very hard to build a positive self-concept in a youngster when the messages are not getting through!

In summation, parents in trouble must look objectively at themselves first. One of the major causes of sagging self-concept in kids today is the fact that parents simply do not spend enough time with their children. Another major cause is that parents, during the time they **do** spend with their youngsters, send far more corrective and negative messages to their kids than positive ones. Perhaps the greatest cause of sagging self-concept in kids is a sagging self-concept in a parent. As the parent(s) change(s), so will the kid(s).

Secondly, parents must discriminate between what they can change and what they can't. Then they must go to work finding positive value in what cannot be changed. Third, parents must establish firm, consistent, and clearly communicated house rules and respond positively when the rules are followed. The **more** positive we are about **followed** rules, the less we will have to ground, deprive, admonish, and punish when they are broken. Finally, we must keep the lines of communication open and keep sending the message of love.

NOTES

Chapter Seven:

TIPS FOR TEACHERS IN TROUBLE

It seems a bleak time for teachers. Discipline, every year for the past ten years, has been named the number one problem facing the schools. Violence, along with the problems of busing, bilingualism, special education mainstreaming, teacher strikes, declining enrollments, closing schools, changing neighborhoods, the rise of drug abuse among students, loss of tax bases, loss of federal programs, and many other problems make education a challenging profession and dramatically different from what it was 10-15 years ago.

Certainly by now, you would be disappointed in me if I could not rattle off all the positive aspects of this grim situation.

Well, look at it this way, teachers. Today, there is nothing boring about our profession. Our jobs offer us incredibly demanding challenges about every two minutes. It is any wonder that occasionally we are carried, like over-stressed air traffic controllers, away from our classrooms on stretchers? Is it any wonder that we suffer a high rate of peptic and duodenal ulcers, heart and cardio-vascular problems, dizziness, nausea, and other stress symptoms, not to mention plain old burnout?

What our communities do not realize (and maybe it is time they should) is that we were given little training in the area of classroom management, and even those of us with years of combat experience in the classroom sometimes have trouble mustering the courage it takes to "face the kids."

Unlike the parents, who rarely have more than two or three at a time to manage, we have thirty-five, forty, and sometimes, on the secondary level, as many as 200 kids in the same room. (Question: How does one build positive self-concepts in 200 kids at the same time? Answer: Very fast, at a speed of 200 mph; say "Good job, nice work, good job, nice work. . .").

Here are some tips to follow. Each tip has an exercise designed to make your job easier, more rewarding, and more self concept building for the kids who depend on you for a great education.

TIP ONE   **Seriously Examine and Try at Least One of the Several Excellent and Commercially Available Classroom Management Systems**.

If you haven't looked lately, or your inservice committee doesn't have the money, then investigate and **pay yourself** for some specific skills training in effective classroom management. There are two reasons why you must do this. In the first place, if you are like most teachers, you haven't been trained adequately and given specific skills to respond appropriately to today's behavior problems. Secondly, you cannot begin to build positive self-concept in kids when your room is in chaos and you spend your day babysitting. The following are some programs you may want to investigate: Dr. Edward Pino's Program, *Discipline Strategies That Work* (ECA, 1979), is an excellent, fully mediated package which will give you a place to start. Dr. James Dobson's book (and tapes), *Dare to Discipline* (Tynedale House, 1970), is still an excellent guide for teaching respect and responsibility to children. Certainly, Dr. William Glasser's approach, *Reality Therapy* (Harper and Row, 1976), has helped thousands of teachers gain control of their lives in the classroom. Without question, the most effective of the classroom management systems is Lee and Marlene Canter's *Assertive Discipline* (Canter and Associates, 1976—available in book, workbook, film, slide tape, and workshop format). The Canters' work re-empowers the classroom teacher to take charge of the educational environment and put him/her in a relatively trouble-free environment in which to work.

Teachers, once our environment is mostly trouble-free, then our real work begins. The purpose of school is to provide a myriad of real learning opportunities for our kids. The reason we want them to learn is so they lead happy, productive, and constructive lives. We do not educate them to be losers at the game of life. If, when they leave us, they have the skills but not the will to use the skills, we have not succeeded.

Exercise for Tip One

Read a book or go to a workshop (preferably **both**) on the subject of classroom management. Then put into practice for a period of **one month** the principles you learned. At the end of the one month period, sit down in a quiet moment and answer these questions:

1. What was good about my classroom management system? (Think **positive!**)

2. What didn't work? What can I do to fix it?

3. Did the kids understand my rules? Should I change my rules?

4. Did I receive support from the administration and parents on my classroom management system? What can I do to get better support? Did I acknowledge those who did support me? (Was I **positive?**)

5. Which of my students have benefited

the most by my classroom management system? How can I let them know I appreciate their support?

6. Did I structure a positive learning environment with my new management system, or did I succeed only in intimidating the kids with a lot of negative consequences which made them feel like prisoners and me feel like a warden?

7. Does my classroom management system give kids opportunities to win? Have I built in sufficient incentives for them to work by themselves, with me, and with others for the purpose of achieving a goal?

8. Does my new management system **help** students develop goals and work toward them, so I have greater opportunities to positively respond to the kids?

9. Does my new classroom management system in any way defeat kids or send them negative messages about themselves and serve to destroy developing positive self-concepts?

One final suggestion on Tip One: If you don't like the first classroom management system you try—try another. The best way to find one that works is to ask your colleagues. They will give it to you straight.

TIP TWO **Be Good to Yourself**

Obviously, you are not going to do a great job of building a positive self-concept in kids if your own self-concept is sagging. Here are some common reasons why a teacher's self-concept sags.

1. Your principal doesn't support you or appreciate your work.

2. You are doing more paperwork and less teaching than you've ever done, and you didn't go to school to be a secretary.

3. You are so tired at the end of the day, you have no time or energy for your own children.

4. The only parents you hear from are the ones who do not like what you are doing.

5. If is wasn't for one or two kids, every day would be great.

6. If is wasn't for one or two kids, every day would be terrible.

7. You know your retirement checks will be pitifully small, and when you retire, social security will be bankrupt. You may have to eat dog food, and you haven't found a brand you like.

8. If one more kid asks to sharpen his/her pencil during a lesson, you will wrap your hands around his/her throat and squeeze the Charmin.

9.   You're afraid to call Tommy's parents because Tommy's father made a pass at one of the other teachers last year (a man).

10.   You're afraid to call Consuela's parents because they don't speak English.

11.   You're afraid to call Marty's parents because his father is the superintendent.

12.   You're afraid to call your own parents because your mother told you not to go into teaching in the first place.

The list goes on and on. I am sure as you read, you thought of a few beauties of your own. Bleak and dismal thoughts and gutwrenching fears will not help you. Such feelings will leave you with a sense of helplessness and "I can't do it," or "I can't take it anymore." The worst is, "Why am I doing this; no one cares." Hence the tip: **Be Good to Yourself.** How can you expect anyone to respect you if you do not respect yourself? Here are ten thoughts to start you on the road to rebuilding your sagging self-concept.

1.   You are an important person.

2.   Your profession is **the** most important profession. Without teachers, there aren't any other professions.

3.   You have spent thousands, maybe hundreds of thousands of hours in the grand and demanding company of kids; **no one** knows your kids as well

as you do.

4.   You have special, unique skills and in-
      sights to impart to kids; they
      desperately need your human love
      and professional care. They will fail
      without you.

5.   In many cultures, what you do is con-
      sidered sacred. In some cultures (unfor-
      tunately not ours anymore) people tip
      their hats and bow to you out of
      respect for your work and dedication.

6.   You are the professional in whose
      company kids will spend more time
      than with any other professional. You
      are their introduction to the world of
      adults beyond that of their parents.

7.   For your kids, you are the embodi-
      ment of authority; you represent what
      is good, what is true, and what is fair
      and just.

8.   By society, you are asked to play more
      roles than any other professional. You
      are a leader, inspirer, minister, dentist,
      nurse, physician, social worker,
      disciplinarian, mother, father, subject-
      matter expert, human and civil rights
      guardian, government representative,
      artist, crafts person, committee
      member, parent-child liaison, jailer,
      dietician, accountant, and milk money
      expert. In the main, you play these han-
      dily, with flair, with a sense of humor,

and **well**.

9.   You are asked to teach kids who
          someday will make more money than
          you, be more powerful than you,
          make more contributions than you
          have, change the course of human
          history, and (even) remove carcinoma
          from your body with a beam of light.
          ("Aren't you Mrs. Marks from the
          Washington School? I remember you.
          Laser, please!")

10.   You are all things to all kids, and more,
          you are worthy of a special name—a
          name that (as some say) God's own son
          was proud to be called by his student,
          Peter, in the Garden of Gethsemani
          when he said, "Hail, Teacher."

Exercise for Tip Two

For teachers in the profession longer than ten years,
here is an excellent activity to bolster a sagging self-
concept. In a quiet and reflective moment, construct a list
(read old grade books or yearbooks for memory jogging)
of all the kids you have taught of whom it could be said
you made **a significant difference** in their lives. Include
on this list all former students who took the time to write
to you after you taught them; all former and present
students who come up to you in the grocery store to smile
and say hello; certainly include all former students that at
the time impressed you as candidates for the local peniten-
tiary, who are now distinguished state senators, or lawyers
and gynecologists in Beverly Hills, Hawaiian real estate
developers, and your own school superintendent.
Remember all the things you said and did to them when

they were "impossible students" and keep on doing it!

For teachers in the profession under ten years, try the following: In a quiet and reflective moment (and if you don't have many of these, we have one clue as to why your self-concept is sagging) construct some **realistic** and achievable rewards for yourself (Example: new dress, glass of rare wine, new golf clubs, etc.) and make them contingent on an improved performance in an area of your life which needs attention. (Example: more education course credit, an improved teacher evaluation, better interpersonal relations with the administration or colleagues, etc.) Then stake out a plan for achieving this goal and get to work. It is truly **wonderful** what winning does for the self-concept!

Remember this lesson from your life the next time you draft an academic or behavioral goal for a kid—nothing helps the self-concept like success—nothing.

TIP THREE   Get the Parents Involved Early.

There are many reasons why teachers fail to seek help from parents early. First, teachers think (erroneously) that calling the parents of a kid in trouble is an admission of their own incompetency. Second, teachers rarely have any ideas when the parents says "What an I supposed to do with him/her?" Third, parents often tend to be defensive, and the teachers do not like battling the defense mechanisms of parents when they need the energy to help the kid. Fourth, many teachers discover from dealing with parents exactly where the kid learned his/her negative self-concept and "loser" mentality. Fifth, some parents are difficult to contact, work long hours, are never home, don't exist, etc., and teachers who have expended unrewarded energy searching for a parent to help, tend to lapse into a "why bother" posture. Sixth, teachers frequently have unhappy or frustrating experiences attempting to work with culturally different parents. They speak little or no English, and using an interpreter is awkward, and done without skill, could lead to an intercultural incident.

The list of reasons for not contacting parents early when there is trouble goes on, but the point remains: **Teacher have a professional obligation to contact parents early when there is trouble**. So here is a list of suggestions for making your contact with parents a positive and rewarding experience for them as well as yourself because this is the first step toward **unifying** the first two ecologies (see Chapter Three) for the purpose of building a positive self-concept in a kid.

1. **Before** you call or send a note to yell and scream to parents about what their kid did in school, send a **positive** note home telling them what an outstanding job their kid did on a particular day. Example: "Dear Mr. & Mrs. Rodriguez: Rosa Linda was a star in mathematics class today. Thanks for your support. You must be wonderful parents!" Now, tell me they are going to be defensive and uncooperative next time you need their help because Rosa Linda is not doing her homework. No way.

2. **Be positive** about the kid when you talk to his/her parents. Remember, it is a scary experience for **all** parents to have to talk to their kid's teacher. So smile, use humor, make them feel relaxed and comfortable by stressing the kid's abilities and positive virtues.

3.   State the problem in very clear
            language. Do not hedge. Don't give
            them the impression that it's nothing
            you can't handle or it's a stage she/he's
            going through, or some other
            minimizer. If the kid is stealing, say
            "Kevin is stealing money from other
            kids in the bathrooms." He says, "Give
            me a quarter, of I'll punch your lights
            out."

4.   Stress how important the kid's self-
            concept is and that a kid whose self-
            concept includes stealing **will** continue
            to **steal for the rest of his/her life**.

5.   Propose a plan for developing a more
            positive self-concept for the kid in
            question. Here you have to teach the
            parents to be more positive with Rosa
            Linda or Kevin: you have to teach
            mom and dad how to "catch them be-
            ing good." **Most** parents do not under-
            stand this principle. If they did, you
            wouldn't be conferencing with them in
            the first place.

6.   Help the parents develop a behavior
            management system at home, one that
            includes rules and positive as well as
            effective negative consequences. Stress
            that it is the positive response, when
            the kids follow the rules, which helps
            build a positive self-concept. Again,
            parents do not understand this princi-
            ple, or they wouldn't be experiencing
            trouble.

7.   When you get evidence that the
parents are responding more positively
to their kid, get on the phone, write a
note and (of course) **thank** them. This
will help their self-concepts, too.

Exercise for Tip Three

Select two of your most troublesome students. Catch
them doing something right this week. Send a brief note
home to their parents describing the good things you
observed. Be sure to thank the parent(s) **in advance** for
"good support." Next time one of these students (or both)
does something you do not like, schedule a parent conference and follow the guidelines for a **positive** parent
conference I listed earlier in the chapter. After the conference and a few days of classroom observation, answer
these questions:

1.   What changes in the kid's behavior
have taken place as a result of my
meeting with his/her parents?

2.   Have I responded positively when I
observed him/her do something I
liked?

3.   Have I responded positively but in an
inappropriate way ("Oh Reggie—[age
15]—I L-L-LOVE how you are working now that your mom and dad and I
have a little—heh! heh!—understanding,") or at an inappropriate time (in
front of the entire class).

4.   What messages has the kid been sending me with his/her body language or

tone of voice? Are these messages telling me I am the enemy?

5.   Did I follow up my conference with a
phone call or note designed to be
positive with them for their support
and to keep the lines of communication open between us?

6.   Did the parents follow up on the training I gave them? Have they positively
responded to desirable behavior, and
have they structured their **time** as well
as material items as rewards and incentives?

7.   Have I been positive, even when
disciplining the kid, so she/he gets the
message I care about him/her as a person even though there are certain
behaviors I will not tolerate?

8.   How many opportunities, **this week**,
has this kid had to **win** at something
and feel good about him/herself? How
could I create more opportunities and
help to engineer success?

9.   How am I feeling about myself since I
have taken the time, energy, and patience to reach out and help parents
and a kid in trouble?

10.   How will I feel about myself as I begin
to see this kid win?

Final note on early parent involvement: remember,

teachers, there's only one thing more important than winning, and even Vince Lombardi knew it—that's having the skill to show somebody else how to win. So spark some teamwork spirit in those parents. Let them know you are on their team, and you have a common goal—the success of their kid. In reality, teacher, you are not only **on** their team, you are the coach! So frequently teachers say, "If only the parents knew what they were doing, we wouldn't have this trouble!" Yet, to whom can the parents turn to for help? **US!** We are the first point of inquiry when parents are in trouble. So we had better be prepared to respond with a winning attitude when they say, "What'll we do now, coach?" Because when we throw in the towel, the match is over, the game is done, and we have lost. When we lose, the kids never have a chance. So, let's go get 'em, team!

TIP FOUR   Consult You Colleagues

It is a rare school these days whose faculty and adminstration are united in their effort to build positive self-concepts in kids. Show me a school where the faculty and adminstration are united in their effort to engineer positive learning experiences for kids, and I will show you a school which produces champions every single time. But so many of us in teaching today are victims of the "little red schoolhouse syndrome." We think we are all alone, by ourselves, the kids against us, and we are incompetent teachers if we cannot do it all by ourselves. Well, the little red schoolhouse is dead. There is a war zone out there, and you don't go into a war zone alone. Get some help. Sit down with your colleagues and trade tricks on sending kids positive messages. Ask the veterans, particularly the ones you all acknowledge as gifted master teachers, and ask very specific questions about their techniques for helping kids feel good about themselves. The more specific your questions, the richer and more accurate the response.

(You will likely discover that many gifted teachers, ironically, have a very difficult time expressing exactly what it is they do when they deal with a kid whose self-concept is very negative. This is understandable when you realize that very few education courses teach specific skills for building self-concept in kids, so what your gifted colleague is doing may be instinctive and never analytically considered or articulated.)

If you really are on fire to develop self-concept building skills, spend some time with a colleague who is a successful and well-respected athletic coach. You will see positive reinforcement in action. You will see enthusiasm, desire, motivation, go-go and win-win mentality at its best. You will see your colleague smile, laugh, joke, jump up and down, tease **in a constructive, image-building, legend-building way** ("Smith? You want to know about Smith? Well for openers the kid is a psychic phenomenon. No joke, he has ESP when it comes to finding the ball carrier. I swear he doesn't open his eyes! But when he tackles somebody, I know he has the ball. Kid never misses.") Did you hear that phrase "kid never misses"? Well, some other people heard it, too. The coach made sure of that. Legends are born this way. Champions are made this way.

Exercise for Tip Four

Sit down with a wise and skillful colleague and ask very specific questions about a specific kid. Find out how your colleague would go about building this kid's self-concept. Take notes and don't say, "It won't work; I tried it." (Don't forget the skills of positive listening and positive talking when working with your colleagues. They need support, too!) Listen particularly for specific rewards your problem kids can earn, like earning the right to be class monitor for Jason, the right to take the attendance cards to the office for Mildred, the right to read first for May Ling, the opportunity to represent the class in a school function for Paul, etc. You will discover from your successful colleagues that among the best rewards for kids are those which **carry** responsibility. The reason is that handling responsibility well is more than its own reward for kids—it is a major builder of self-confidence.

To summarize tips for teachers in trouble: Teachers today are presented with overwhelming problems and constant stress. Unless we are able to feel good about ourselves and the job we are doing, we will not be effective role models for kids. In order to feel good about ourselves, we must first get some strong classroom management skills. Furthermore, we must not use those skills to trounce kids. Rather, we must develop positive classroom management skills to consistently reinforce kids for doing what we want them to do.

Secondly, we must be good to ourselves by realizing that while society asks us to do a very time-consuming and physically/mentally demanding task, we are special and talented human beings capable of meeting that challenge. We are the backbone of the most moral and good aspects of our society.

Thirdly, we must work with parents, early and often, in order to secure a more positive and self-concept building case for kids. And we must realize that unless we train the parents to catch the kids being good, no one else will.

Finally, we must realize that we are not alone in our work with kids. We must frequently and assiduously call on our colleagues for new and practical ways of sending positive messages to kids. As teachers we must realize that never was it more apparent that the future is firmly, positively, and irrevocably in our hands, and **WE ARE NEEDED**.

NOTES

Chapter Eight:

TIPS FOR BUILDING POSITIVE PEER MESSAGES FOR APPROPRIATE BEHAVIOR IN KIDS

You may recall that in an earlier discussion I said that the third ecology (the kid and his/her friends) is the most powerful ecology of all. The need to have friends who are loving, respecting, and approving is great in all of us. Therefore, much of our behavior is designed to win the love, respect, and approval of our friends. This is true of kids as well. In fact, it is more true of kids than it is of adults because kids are undergoing tremendous physiological and psychological changes in short periods of time. They are constantly discovering themselves, rediscovering themselves, and testing their own limitations. As they play new roles, experiment with new activities, and adopt new postures, they embark on a ceaseless search for acceptance and approval. They quickly learn that certain behaviors attract them friends and, in some cases, admirers. They fear, by the seventh grade, they will be thought of as "weird," or a "goody-goody" or, the absolute worst, (at this writing) "queer." Middle school or junior high teachers, who have experience teaching at the elementary levels as well, will tell you that the tremendous difference between elementary and junior high age kids is the intensification of the socialization process at the junior high levels. Naturally, with this intensification comes a need for greater acceptance as well as greater accessibility to the group. Bathroom humor, popular in the fifth and sixth grade, begins to fade, and sexual humor, with great emphasis on boy-girl differences, becomes the preoccupation of the group. The key to survival can be expressed in the question, "What can I do or say that will attract to me others who will help me get my needs met?"

Rather than be threatened by this intensification of socialization in our kids (as parents frequently are) or punished by it (as teachers many times are), we must begin to understand that kids of all ages have strong social needs and must get them met in order to be happy. Show me an unhappy kid, and I **won't** show you a kid who's worried over bad grades; instead I'll show you a kid whose friend wants to play with someone else today, whose friends forgot to invite her to the party, who was not invited to the dance, who did not make the team, who has no date for the prom, whose pimples have blossomed like roses in June. In short, show me an unhappy kid, and I'll show you a social loser in the game of life.

Yet, as parents we fail to teach our children simple (but terribly important) socialization skills and worse, as teachers, we systematically punish them for being social, because, teachers say, they choose to be social at the wrong times. Many times we fail to teach kids the minimum skills they need to survive in a world of others who need as much or more reinforcement than they do. One reason we do is that we are so busy attending to our own social needs, we forget the needs of our kids. How important it is for kids to learn the difference between people who love you for you and people who love you because you fit their agendas. How important it is for our kids to learn the difference between people who are "givers" and people who are "takers"—between people who are "helpers" and people who are "users."

Until our kids learn these "life" lessons, they are prey to their own needs for love, acceptance, and approval. The world is filled with predators, some of whom act consciously and others who unwittingly destroy and hurt many of the people they touch.

All of this boils down to a critical skill our kids must have in order to survive in the strange world we live in today. The skill is picking and choosing friends. Most parents, as they do with matters of discipline, **react** to the friends their children choose: they either like them, or they don't. Few parents go beyond the stage of expressing their likes and dislikes until some trouble develops. "You were caught what? Shoplifting! Oh my God, I don't believe this. You were with that Maxwell girl, weren't you? I told you she was bad news, didn't I?" "That Maxwell girl" may very well be bad news, mom, but tell me this: did you ever sit down with your daughter and have a non-threatening and plainly instructive chat about what to look for in picking a friend?

Teachers, who spend many hours of their days observing friendship and patterns of influence among kids, are an excellent resource for parents who want to know about their children's friends. We watch so many "nice kids" in school come under the irresistible influence of others who send those powerful "I like you; you're a neat person" messages for the **wrong** reasons. Kids who normally draw so little of that reinforcement from home and teachers at school are so vulnerable to that message of support they will do anything, virtually anything, to improve, augment, and maintain those messages of regard from their friends.

Consider, too, that this third ecology includes a special group called siblings. Siblings are special peers in that they participate in the home ecology, may participate in the school ecology (depending on age difference), and participate in the peer ecology as well. Instinctively, parents recognize the special place occupied by siblings—"You keep an eye on your brother, understand? I don't want him in any more trouble." Siblings are the members of the peer ecology over which parents should realize they have a measure of control.

My point is that the place to begin is for parents and teachers to realize that we have the potential for exercising much greater influence in the peer ecology than we commonly recognize. Here are some tips for parents, to be followed by tip for teachers, for the purpose of exercising more influence over the kinds of messages our kids' friends are sending them about their behavior.

PARENT TIP ONE **Know Your Children's Friends.**

Go out of your way to get them in your life, if only for brief but meaningfully shared experiences. Family parties, picnics, outings, camping trips, special occasions send out the message: **you are welcome here**. Send them the positive messages you are sending your children, and you will get to know them well. In fact, if you go overboard on the positives for your children's friends, you will need an addition on the house. They will never go home!

PARENT TIP TWO **Do Not Cross-Examine Your Children's Friends.**

If they suspect that they are invited for the purpose of information-gathering and scrutiny, they will evaporate like dew on a desert morning. Questions like, "What does your father do for a living, Janet?" may be harmless enough, but the game of "twenty-questions" grows old for kids, and they get a very negative message from interrogation.

PARENT TIP THREE **Watch For the Behavior Your Children's Friends Encourage in Your Children; Watch For the Behavior Your Children Encourage in Their Friends.**

Understanding the motivating factors behind everyday decisions your children make is easier when you realize that they are participating in a circle of friends and acquaintences which has a behavior code of its own. This code may embrace some of your own values; then again, it may embrace values foreign and threatening to your own. Observing the messages your children's friends send them will not only help you understand your children's behavior, it will help you assess the relative strength of their self-concepts as they invariably compare themselves to their friends. Remember, they have to be happy in their **own** world. In order to survive without serious scars, psychological traumas, and emotional setbacks, they have to follow the rules of their own world. Conflicts with you may arise when your world's values have no meaning or have a negative meaning for your children. One way to understand their world is to be vigilant about messages of regard which they exchange. If they reward one another for wearing certain shirts, jeans, blouses, or shoes because they are "in," then we must understand that as parents we are presented with an opportunity. Most parents **miss** the opportunity. Because the "in" clothes inevitably cost more, some parents are outraged. "Why should I pay $21.95 for this shirt because it has that silly logo, when I can buy the same thing at K-Mart for $8.95?"

The "when I was your age" lecture may very well justify **to you** why you refuse to submit to pressure; it doesn't help them in their attempt to fit into their own world. Their friends and acquaintances may very well brutalize them for living by your values in their world. Now, of course, if their self-concepts are so strong and self-assured that they can laugh in the face of peer derision, then you have done a great job and very well may have a **trend setter** for a son or daughter. But if they lack the self-assurance to effectively deal with peer derision (kids can be very cruel; they learn from us), then you have set them up. They walk into a potentially harmful world defenseless and wearing red flags and the scent of the victim. After getting chewed-up, roughed-up, and hurt by their peers, they will develop a rather sophisticated set of defense mechanisms. Some of these will irritate you.

"How come he spends so much time in his room lately?"
"All she does is come home, get something to eat, and go
into her room and listen to her stereo." "She just will not
eat. I suppose she's worried about being overweight. But,
Lord, she's thin as a stick. She refuses to eat. When she
does, I think she makes herself throw-up." "He just quit
school. And he was getting good grades. One day he just
quit."

Now, I am **not** suggesting to parents that they buy
every little whim, give in on every issue, turn over the
checkbook to the kid—far from it. I am suggesting that
understanding the circumstances **behind** the behavior
(particularly the peer pressure) gives you an excellent opportunity to build a positive self-concept in a youngster.
Witness: "Jeffrey, I understand the situation. All your
friends wear alligator shirts. You like them, too. But they
cost six and a half dollars more than the same shirt without
the alligator. Here's the deal. I think you are number one,
and you should wear the best. So, you will have to earn
the difference between the cost of the shirts. I pay a dollar
an hour for window cleaning, leaf raking, and babysitting
your brother and sister."

Now Jeffrey has an opportunity to wear the clothes he
wants to feel comfortable among his friends—furthermore, he has great incentive to work! His shirts take on a
new meaning. They now symbolize his responsibility to
himself. Do you think you will find them crumpled in a
ball in the bottom of his closet? More than likely, you will
find the shirts he spent six and a half hours **each** working
for will get hung neatly in a closet or folded in his drawer.
Before long he will request, mom, that you iron them
(even though they are perma-press). Remembering the formula for positive self-concept, you take the opportunity
to say, "I am impressed that you care enough about your
appearance to want ironed shirts. Since I don't have time

to iron them myself, I would be happy to teach you to iron them." He will—of course. Again, another opportunity to feel good about himself, and haven't you taught him a wonderful lesson about life? You want it; you work for it. All this because instead of screaming, "I don't care what your friends are wearing, I'm not etc., etc." or saying, "Iron perma-press? You need your head examined!" or worse, "Sure I'll iron them for you, honey." By realizing the messages Jeffrey's friends are sending him, we help Jeffrey win.

But his friends aren't the only ones sending messages; he's sending them back. By watching these, you will learn an enormous amount about **yourself**. Is he mean to his friends? Moody with his friends? Tease them to the point of pain? Use them for his own ends? Or is he supportive of their needs and sharing? Is he polite with them? Does he encourage them to try? Does he help them win? Whatever messages he sends, mom and dad, remember this: how he treats them is exactly what he learned from you.

PARENT TIP FOUR **Periodically Discuss Your Children's Friends With Your Children.**

Now, the worst thing you can do is give the impression that **you** are evaluating and making decisions about your kid's friends. Don't do it. What you want is for the kid to have the skill to evaluate and make decisions about his/her own friends. Because friendship is so important to all of us, it has become almost a "scared cow." Yes, we believe it is a basic human right to choose our own friends. Of course it is. Friends who hurt us for their own ends are not friends. Face it, mom and dad, it's one of life's toughest lessons. Just who are our friends, anyway? So your discussions with your kids about friends should give your kids the freedom to draw their **own** conclusions. You can lead the discussion to cover points about goals, objectives, healthy activities, dangerous activities, and don't forget those self-concept messages: friends who send self-concept crippling messages **are not friends**, and when they are lovers, the relationship will never last. If by chance it does, it can never be healthy, and unhealthy relationships have a way of producing troubled kids. Thus, the cycle of defeat is complete. By responding positively to each other and our children, we boldly break that destructive cycle.

Tips For Teachers

As teachers, we have a major advantage over parents when it comes to observing peer message systems shape kids. We see it happening every day in our classrooms, in the halls, in the recess yard and cafeteria, in the parking lot, and at "the gathering place for trouble"—almost every school has one. We regularly and daily observe the social interaction of the kids. In fact, we see so much of it, we become inured to the psychological destruction that may happen under our noses. We hear them "cut up" each other, listen to cruel and judgmental nicknames, observe them in potentially dangerous and image-compromising behavior, and **we say or do nothing**.

We can channel the energy they have to hurt each other into activities which will teach them mutual respect. Futhermore, we can structure those activities to teach them to be more supportive of each other with activities which enhance rather than interfere with our lessons and actually train the kids to send self-concept building messages to each other. Here are some tips to help you design such activities for your particular classroom and school.

TEACHER TIP ONE   Make Rules Which Prohibit the Exchange of Overt

Negative Messages Among the Kids.

Beyond the obvious rules like "no fighting," "no name-calling or teasing," and "do not destroy the property of others," you can add rules like "no nicknames," no "obscene language or **gestures**," or "say or do nothing which could hurt or offend another person's feelings."

Once you have developed these rules, **enforce them**, and don't say "we can't do that at our school" and sound like a loser. Be a winning teacher, and do something about it when Marvin calls Carrie "the lip" and everybody laughs. Remember if you do not enforce the rules, your rules are a waste of time. Also remember that the best way to enforce the rules is to catch a kid observing them. "Marvin, I noticed that you called everyone today by their first name. I appreciate it, Marvin. You're super!"

TEACHER TIP TWO Don't Punish The Group For The Errors of A Few.

It seems obvious to include this tip, but many teachers use the technique of punishing the group for the mistakes of a few. The Marines may claim this technique builds group spirit, but it doesn't. It does lead to the group, behind the barracks and at night, throwing a blanket over the head of the offender and beating him to a bloody pulp. In schools this technique leads to the exchange of negative and self-concept shattering messages.

In response to this tip, some teachers will say, "But what do you do if you don't know who did it?" The answer to this question lies in the following illustration of group rewards:

Pino, Glasser, the Canters (see Chapter

Seven), and others all detail excellent models for classwide reward systems. The point of their use is that they unequivocally promote group collaboration, cohesion, and the exchange of positive information between students **for doing what you want them to do**. Example: a teacher who offers the class a reward of listening to their favorite radio station for five minutes at the **end** of class **if** they earn forty "bonus" points during the class, has a very sophisticated (and easy-to-execute) behavior management tool at his/her disposal. The kids win these "bonus" points at the **sole** discretion of the teacher. She/he awards them as she/he catches kids in the act of **following the rules** and making contributions to the general welfare of the class. Students whose peers previously "egged them on" by laughing and generally admiring them for destroying the learning atmosphere, now send them **glances of approval** as they win bonus points toward "the prize." Of course, they must win, and they must want the prize. You, teacher, engineer the win by awarding the final point (to the **worst** behavior problem, of course), ten seconds prior to the last five minutes of the class period. Now, the worst behavior problem, who is the one with the lowest self-concept, naturally is **cheered** by his/her friends for doing what you wanted him/her to do. If you are clever enough to offer a "three-minute bonus on the radio" if there are no rules broken during the class, then you do not have to "see" them to catch the rule breaker. When you later hear the disruption you announce, calmly, the loss of the bonus. The kids will look directly at the offender and you will know who caused the trouble. This way you monitor the class without "watching" them. Of course, whatever you do to the offender is not nearly the punishment she/he receives as the class stares in silence in his/her direction. If you haven't seen this phenomenon in action (and I can't imagine you haven't), it is a graphic demonstration of the power of the peer ecology. Because you are a **positive** teacher, you will strive to help them win. (I suggest that the student whose disruption lost the bonus be the student whose behavior earns the last few bonus points for the first part of the reward so she/he is redeemed in the eyes of his/her friends.)

TEACHER TIP THREE   Use Peer Teaching.

I am astonished at how little my colleagues rely on one of the greatest and most easily obtainable resources in our classrooms today—the kids themselves. A lot of reliable research on peer teaching says it is a highly effective teaching technique. What the research doesn't point out is what peer teaching does to self-concept. In the first place, it allows the teacher to publicly recognize students with special subject matter knowledge and skills (positive messages from the first ecology). Secondly, it allows the student to tell his/her parents of the special recognition as she/he prepares the lesson at home. Of course, positive parents will respond appropriately (positive messages from the second ecology). Thirdly, it permits the student to help his/her classmates to learn from one of their own, which is especially rewarding when a certain prize has been offered if all students score above a certain grade on the test, complete a special assignment, etc. (positive messages from the third ecology). Of course, the teacher, freed from the pressure of delivering the lesson, is free to pay more attention to the process of positive self-concept development, which, as any teacher will tell you, is one of the greatest joys of our profession, and on this point, I end the final chapter of this book, but please do read on!

NOTES

Epilogue:

NEVER TOO LATE TO BEGIN

"In the morning sow thy seed, and in the
evening let not thy hand cease, for thou
knowest not which may spring up, this
or that; and if both together, it
shall be better."

Ecclesiastes 11, 6

I have to believe as William Faulkner said so well when he accepted the Nobel Prize for literature, "Man will endure." I have to believe that we will endure because we have the power to change, and I also believe that we can never change the behavior of someone else unless we ourselves are willing to change. When we demonstrate our ability to change to kids, we teach them a powerful lesson about life. We teach them that they have the power to do virtually anything they want to do—be anything they want to be.

Kids are forever. They are at once our joy and our frustration. They are Hamlet's mirror held up to ourselves. For nothing angers us more than seeing our own faults in our children. Nothing pleases us more than hearing another say something nice about our kids. Because they grow up with us and we—is it not true?—grow up with them, we know each other's sources of pleasure and pain. Who can hurt you more than your mother? And who, with a word or two or a sentence in a letter, can make you weep silent tears of joy? Why, in the cartoon, does the psychiatrist thoughtfully stroke his beard and say, "Tell me about your mother"?

Why, teacher, does the memory of a certain student stay with us forever? Don't we get that special shot of joy when they come back after long years with that look-what-I've-done-with-my-life-and-thank-you look? It needs no words.

I have tried in this book to speak to you from my heart and say things I have spent long hours thinking about, reading about, talking about, teaching about, probably—you'll smile—preaching about because as an athlete, teacher, parent, and professional helper, I see winners and losers every day. And while they all pretty much look the same, they do not act the same, and they certainly do not speak the same language. The language of lose is replete with the words "I can't," "I won't," and "why bother?" The language of win uses words like "I can," "I will," and "why not?"

The language of lose in the mouth of a derelict, convict, or terrorist is understandable, indeed. But the language of lose in the mouth of a kid is crushing. When you hear it, you always wonder what a toll forty, fifty, or sixty years of losing will take on this kid as well as on the innocent bystanders in the accident of his/her life. It is we who teach them how to talk.

Now, the language of win is music in the mouth of a child. It first tinkles like a wind harp in a light breeze; it is a prelude to the thundering overture of a great life filled with the sound and fury signifying **something**. That something is why we must believe we will endure. Let us teach them the language of win. Let us feed their souls with "I can" and "I will" and "why not?" Let the language of win help them grow strong in their own eyes. For it is never to late to begin. For them and the generations which follow, we can offer no greater gift.

Thank you for reading my book and GO GET 'EM.

NOTES

NOTES

TEACHERS: Use this chart as a model for your classroom. Fill it in, print it on large poster board. Post it **in front** of your classroom, and **use it every day**.

THE ZINK METHOD

CLASS RULES
1. _____
2. _____
3. _____
4. _____
5. _____

REWARDS (What happens when you follow the rules!)
1. _____
2. _____
3. _____

NEGATIVE CONSEQUENCES (What you choose by breaking one or more of the rules.)
1. A verbal warning
2. Loss of a privilege for a short time
3. _____

Remember: Negative consequences do not promote good behavior; they stop bad behavior. Positive consequences promote good behavior. So catch them being good!

GO GET' EM!

PARENTS: Cut out, fill in duplicate, and post at least three places:
1) The refrigerator   2) The bathroom, and 3) The kids' rooms.

THE ZINK METHOD

HOUSE RULES

1. _____

2. _____

3. _____

4. _____

5. _____

REWARDS (What happens when you follow the rules!)

1. _____

2. _____

3. _____

NEGATIVE CONSEQUENCES (What you choose by breaking one or more of the rules.)

1. A verbal warning

2. Loss of a privilege for a short time

3. _____

Remember: Negative consequences do not promote good behavior; they stop bad behavior. Positive consequences promote good behavior. So catch them being good!

You are the most important person in you child's life, so put some passion and enthusiasm into your praise!

GO GET' EM!

APPENDIX C

THE KNOW YOUR CHILD GAME.

DIRECTIONS: TAKE THE FOLLOWING QUIZ. THEN, CHECK YOUR ANSWERS WITH YOUR CHILD. SCORE FIVE POINTS FOR EACH CORRECT ANSWER AND TALLY YOUR SCORE.

PERFORMANCE: 80—100 POINTS=CHAMPION PARENT
60—80 POINTS=KNOWLEDGEABLE PARENT
40—60 POINTS=ABSENTEE PARENT
20—40 POINTS=ME GENERATION PARENT
0—20 GET BUSY NOW

FOR SPECIAL FUN, AFTER YOU TAKE THE TEST HAVE YOUR CHILDREN TAKE THE TEST SUBSTITUTING THE WORD "CHILD" WITH THE WORD "PARENT."

1. WHAT IS YOUR CHILD'S FAVORITE TYPE OF MUSIC?__
   _____

2. WHAT IS YOUR CHILD'S FAVORITE MUSICAL ARTIST OR GROUP? _____

3. WHERE WOULD YOUR CHILD CONSIDER A PERFECT PLACE FOR A VACATION?_____

4. WHICH ONE OF **YOUR** FRIENDS DOES YOUR CHILD LIKE BEST?_____

5. WHICH OF **YOUR** FRIENDS DOES YOUR CHILD DISLIKE MOST? _____

6. WHAT ARE THE PHONE NUMBERS OF TWO OF YOUR CHILD'S FRIENDS?_____

7. WHERE DID YOUR CHILD SPEND THE LAST THREE NIGHTS BETWEEN SIX AND TEN PM?_____
   _____

8. WHAT IS YOUR CHILD'S FAVORITE TELEVISION PROGRAM?_____

9. WHAT IS YOUR CHILD'S FAVORITE FOOD?_____

10. WHAT IS THE TITLE OF THE LAST BOOK YOUR CHILD READ? _____

11. WHAT IS THE TITLE OF THE LAST MOVIE YOUR CHILD HAS SEEN?_____

12. HOW MUCH MONEY DOES YOUR CHILD HAVE IN HIS/HER ROOM RIGHT NOW?_____
    NOTE: SCORE FIVE POINTS IF YOUR ANSWER IS WITHIN $3.

13. GIVE YOUR CHILD'S PET NAME FOR ONE OF HIS/HER SIBLINGS AND/OR FRIENDS._____

14. GIVE YOUR CHILD'S PET NAME FOR YOU._____

15. GIVE YOUR CHILD'S PET NAME FOR YOUR SPOUSE.__

16. NAME YOUR CHILD'S FAVORITE TEACHER._____

17. NAME ONE THING YOUR CHILD WOULD **LOVE** TO OWN. _____

18. WHAT DOES YOUR CHILD WANT TO BE WHEN HE/SHE IS GROWN—UP?_____

19. NAME YOUR CHILD'S FAVORITE COLOR AND FAVORITE TOY._____

20. IF YOUR CHILD HAD TO PICK A COLLEGE OR UNIVERSITY RIGHT NOW, WHICH ONE WOULD IT BE?_____

THE CHAMPIONS SERIES
by
Dr. J. Zink

BOOK ONE: $9.95
Praised by teachers and parents as the most straight-forward and easy to read approach to positive discipline, **Building Positive Self-Concept in Kids** will give you hundreds of good ideas for making your relationship with kids a positive experience. This book will train you to build a step-by-step positive discipline plan.

BOOK TWO: $9.95
Motivation problems? Discipline problems? Drug, Alcohol & Teen Sex problems? This book will give you answers! Written in an easy-to-understand style, **Motivating Kids** will give you novel and effective solutions to the bewildering array of troubles that parents and teachers face today.

BOOK THREE: $9.95
EGO STATES is the culmination of the champions trilogy. Here Dr. Zink explains why we lose our tempers, harbor anger, and engage in self-destructive behaviors which further erode our self-esteem. Here are the EXACT steps to take to become more loving and feel more competent as parents and teachers. Whatever you do, don't miss this one!

DEARLY BELOVED: SECRETS OF SUCCESSFUL MARRIAGE $19.95-(Hardbound Only)
Working on the theme of three parts in marriage (sex, intimacy, and commitment) and drawing on his experience in private practice, Dr. Zink departs from his usual subject of child behavior to focus on marriage. Written to celebrate their 21st wedding anniversary, **Dearly Beloved** includes commentory by Dr. Zink's wife, Kern. Here are their secrets of their successful marriage spelled out in plain talk. Don't be married without it!

THE AUDIO TAPE: $14.95

Hear Dr. Zink explain how certain messages destroy and certain messages build a positive self-concept in children and young adults. A motivating and emotional experience, this one hour tape will get you charged up and on a positive track for getting kids to behave. This tape will teach you to follow-through on a positive discipline plan for home or school.

Video Tape One For Parents: The Rules $34.95

Here Dr. Zink describes the very specifics that positive parents use to write the rules for the behavior of their children. This no-nonsense approach includes help for divorced and blended families. (VHS only)

Video Tape Two For Parents: The Prices $34.95

This tape teaches what positive parents do and say when the kids break the rules. Prices are not punishment, Dr. Zink shows clearly, and when you learn this special skill, you are on your way to being a positive parent. (VHS only)

Video Tape Three For Parents: The Positives $34.95

Catching our kids following the rules is what we all know we should do. Here Dr. Zink shares the secrets of the most positive parents as they develop a loving, positive, and powerfully fulfilling relationship with their children. It is never too late to begin! (VHS only)

Video Tape Four For Parents: The Zink Money System $34.95

Thousands of parents have been thrilled with the remarkable effectiveness of this system which replaces allowances for kids with an efficient method for teaching the value of money while building self-worth. (VHS only)

Video Tape Five For Teachers: Classroom Discipline $99.95

Here is the tape educators have been waiting for! Eighty minutes crammed with hundreds of useful ideas organized into a simple system for effective classroom discipline! No one can motivate teachers like Dr. J. Zink. (VHS only)

Video Tape Six For Teachers: The Most Asked
Questions On Discipline. $99.95

In this live session, today's classroom teachers ask Dr. Zink many of the penetrating and very relevant questions facing educators concerned with discipline. Witty and poignant, some of Dr. Zink's answers may surprise even veterans. (VHS only)

THE COMPLETE CHAMPIONS WORKSHOP
AUDIO TAPE: $49.95

And introducing for the first time ever, the complete Dr. J. Zink CHAMPIONS WORKSHOP on audio tape! **Three hours** of fun and fulfillment. On March 5th, 1986, Dr. Zink gave what many consider to be the finest workshop of his professional life to 500 educators in La Porte, Indiana. Here, for the first time, is the complete sound track to that workshop. Dr. Zink, in his own humorous style, teaches his ENTIRE POSITIVE DISCIPLINE PROGRAM on high quality audio cassettes. You will laugh, cry, and learn how to get YOUR needs met while raising and teaching kids!

THE ZINK BULLSEYE CHART: $12.95

Here is the famous Bullseye Chart that has proven so effective in raising academic and behavior performance in kids. 22X34 inches, this plastic-coated, **reusable** progress grade chart teaches kids how to track their own progress. It is ready to hang on the back of their bedroom doors and raise those grades!

THE GUIDES: $3.95 (each)

Champions on the School Bus and **Champions in the Library**. These guides for positive discipline were written specifically for school bus drivers and librarians. In very clear language, these unique pamphlets describe specific techniques to help kids feel good about themselves for behaving on the bus and in the library. No school bus and no library should be without one.

You will believe you can make champions.

Dr. Zink, please send:

_____	Copy(s) BOOK I (Self-Concept)	@	$ 9.95	= $ _____
_____	Copy(s) BOOK II (Motivation)	@	$ 9.95	= $ _____
_____	Copy(s) BOOK III (Ego States)	@	$ 9.95	= $ _____
_____	Copy(s) DEARLY BELOVED (Secrets of Successful Marriage)	@	$19.95	= $ _____
_____	Copy(s) CHAMPIONS AUDIO TAPE	@	$14.95	= $ _____
_____	Copy(s) CHAMPIONS VIDEO TAPES	@ $	_____	= $ _____

Specify Tape Numbers _____

_____	Copy(s) THE COMPLETE CHAMPIONS WORKSHOP AUDIO TAPE	@	$49.95	= $ _____
_____	Copy(s) SCHOOL BUS	@	$ 3.95	= $ _____
_____	Copy(s) LIBRARY	@	$ 3.95	= $ _____
_____	Copy(s) ZINK BULLSEYE CHART	@	$12.95	= $ _____

Total Cost of Material Ordered $ _____

Shipping & Handling (10% of total cost; $3.00 min.) $ _____

Shipping & Hanldling outside U.S.A. (10% of total cost; $5.00 min.) $ _____

CA Residents only: Add 6½% of total cost $ _____

Total amount enclosed $ _____

ORDER MUST BE ACCOMPANIED BY PAYMENT IN FULL. SCHOOL DISTRICTS: PURCHASE ORDER IS OK.

Make check payable to:

    J. ZINK, INC.
    P.O. BOX 3279
    MANHATTAN BEACH, CA 90266

PLEASE SHIP MY MATERIALS TO: (PRINT)

_____

NAME

_____

STREET & ADDRESS

_____

CITY   STATE   ZIP

Note: For VIEDO TAPE VHS format only.

THE CHAMPIONS WORKSHOP

The **CHAMPIONS WORKSHOP** is guaranteed to be a most enlightening and motivating experience for all professional educators, paraprofessionals, support staff, and parents. New and experienced alike will benefit from this program.

This highly acclaimed and proven method of positive child discipline is presented by Dr. J. Zink, creator and developer of the method, and not by trainees or staff members.

Dr. Zink's manner of presentation, a compelling mix of valuable information, wit, humor and poignant examples, captures the heart and mind of virtually every participant, including even the strongest of skeptics.

The **CHAMPIONS WORKSHOP** has been praised and endorsed by those fortunate enough to have attended one. This experience has been credited with: motivating and inspiring careers; changing lives; improving student behavior; elevating student academic performance; changing schools and even entire school systems; and enriching the quality of life of teachers, parents, and kids.

Dr. Zink's legion of admirers and advocates continues to grow for one basic reason . . . The Zink Method of Positive Discipline Works!